Warning: I[...] reached the [...] has record[...] ficult places [...] a "category" [...] one person, [...]

[...] you've [...] ances Bowley [...] nen from dif- [...] ncerned with [...] of us is only [...] Mary Frances.

—**SANDRA STANLEY**, wife, mom, foster care mom, blogger; sandrastanley.com

My work in impoverished neighborhoods has forced me to understand the power and necessity of partnerships in any effort for effective community transformation—no one person or group can have a systemic effect alone. *Make It Zero* inspires us to work together to create communities that truly impact poverty and address the myriad of needs that face those who are most at risk.

—**DANNY WUERFFEL**, executive director, Desire Street Ministries; winner of the 1996 Heisman Trophy

As a culture, it is vital that we do all we can to protect and strengthen the next generation. Through *Make It Zero*, you'll be informed of factors that put our children at risk, inspired by heroes who have overcome the risks, and receive tangible actions you can take to reduce the number of vulnerable children to zero.

—**MARK BATTERSON**, author of *The Circle Maker*, lead pastor of National Community Church

The importance of *Make It Zero* is that it expresses the hope of the issue of human trafficking, while having the audacity to take God at His Word and believe that we can safeguard every child. Mary Frances Bowley is a treasured friend of mine, and her heart to reach out and bring the loving hand of Christ to see children set free from all these profound crimes, and to prevent it in others, is very real. I love her for it. A must-read.

—**DR. BROOK BELLO**, author of *Living Inside the Rainbow*, CEO of More Too Life, and survivor of domestic minor sex trafficking.

Make It Zero eliminates any doubt that every child has the potential to thrive if we are willing to make the most basic investments—food, shelter, health, education and safety—required to nurture and love them. At a time when so many are cynical about our society's ability to solve problems, this book demonstrates the power that faith and resilience have to change lives, communities, and even the world. One story in particular, that of WNBA star Ruth Riley, leapt off the page for me because I've seen firsthand through her work with Share Our Strength how she has drawn on her own life and faith to help others. This is a book with inspiration to be found on every page.

—**BILLY SHORE**, CEO, No Kid Hungry, nokidhungry.org

Make It Zero combines heart-wrenching yet inspiring real-life stories and all the work Mary Frances Bowley has dedicated her life to do: protect and cherish our children. This book empowers all of us to not accept abuse or exploitation and to do everything we can to empower the most vulnerable.

—**KYRA PHILLIPS**, CNN anchor

As the CEO of Randstad, it is our mission to shape the world of work. Through our partnership with Wellspring Living, we have had the opportunity to empower young women toward sustainable employment. Securing a living wage is vital to breaking the cycle of poverty. In *Make It Zero*, you will read stories of these brave young women and those who have been a part of their journey. You will be invited to do something! It will be a decision you will not regret.

—**LINDA GALIPEAU**, CEO Randstad North America

Our children need us in more profound ways than ever before. This book, and particularly the chapter by Dr. Donna Beegle, is a thought-provoking, action-oriented assessment of where we are and how we can respond to the needs of our children. Our words of love and protection for students must be backed up with our policies, institutions, and communities. Dr. Beegle provides a compelling path forward based personally and socially. This is an important read.

—**DR. RUSSELL LOWERY-HART**, president, Amarillo College

Prepare to have your eyes opened, your heart changed, and your mind inspired to do something to make the world a safer place for children. This book challenges all of us to begin the ripple effect of change that this generation desperately needs.

—**NICOLE BRADDOCK BROMLEY**, author of *Hush, Breathe*, and *Soar*; international voice on child sexual abuse and trafficking and founder of OneVOICE (www.iamonevoice.org) and OneVOICE4freedom (www.onevoice4freedom.org)

The person who reads *Makes It Zero* takes step one of relieving oppression—relieving ignorance. *Make It Zero* breaks down the world's seemingly insurmountable problems by connecting and personalizing them. In a society with issues so complicated the logical answer would be despair, this book provides answers in a practical, easy-to-read format. There is hope, but only if we embrace the realities of this text.

—**MARY KATHERINE FECHTEL**, Miss Florida, 2015–16

One child in poverty . . . one child hungry . . . one child lonely . . . one child abused . . . one child trafficked. The fact is there are thousands who every day experience this type of hurt and pain but one is too many. Mary Frances not only inspires us as a community of people but she gives practical steps and real-life stories on how to *Make It Zero*. This book is not only a must-read, it is a rich vision that we must apply as we fight together to Make It Zero.

—**DUSTIN WILLIS**, author of *Life in Community*, coauthor of *Life on Mission*, director of events at the North American Mission Board

Trafficking is a huge problem in the U.S. and around the world. It can be overwhelming to think about what to do to end trafficking and protect those who are most vulnerable. Make It Zero helps you to put your thoughts into action by providing tools, resources, and stories to help equip you and your community. Let *Make It Zero* guide you as we all work together to protect the children.

—**AMENA BROWN OWEN**, spoken word poet, speaker, and author of *Breaking Old Rhythms: Answering the Call of a Creative God*

One of my most prayed prayers is, "God, would You please rescue some kids today? Show me how to help somehow." This book is an answer to those prayers. Often, the sheer amount of evil and darkness that so many children experience in this world paralyzes us into believing that there isn't anything big enough we could do to help. But *Make It Zero* instilled in me a deeper understanding of my responsibility to live with eyes wide open to the needs of children around me. And to find something in my own sphere of influence and faithfully do that one thing.

—**MAGGIE PAULUS**, author of *Finding God at the Kitchen Sink*, blogger at MaggiePaulus.com

There's a plaque over our entry room closet: Home Is Where Your Story Begins. I put it there as our three sons were growing up to remind me of the importance of the home environment. Several years after our youngest went to college we had the privilege of inviting a teenager to call our home hers. Today she is a student at a major university, having escaped what many imagined would be her inescapable future. As we saw how her life changed I decided I should add something to that plaque: Home Is Where Your Story Begins . . . But It Doesn't Have to End There. Read *Make It Zero* and you'll be convinced *you* can make a difference in someone's life; regardless of where the story begins, it can have a positive ending.

—**KENDRA SMILEY**, inspiring speaker and author of the popular three-book Parenting Like a Pro series: *Do Your Kids a Favor. Love Your Spouse*; *Be the Parent*; and *Journey of a Strong-Willed Child*.

make it zero

THE MOVEMENT TO
SAFEGUARD EVERY CHILD

MARY FRANCES BOWLEY

WITH JENNIFER BRADLEY FRANKLIN

MOODY PUBLISHERS

CHICAGO

© 2016 by
WELLSPRING LIVING, INC.

All stories in this book are true. However, to protect privacy, some names and other identifying details have been altered.

Edited by Pam Pugh
Interior and Cover Design: Erik M. Peterson
Author Photo: Sara Hanna Photography

All websites and phone numbers listed herein are accurate at the time of publication but may change in the future or cease to exist. The listing of website references and resources does not imply publisher endorsement of the site's entire contents. Groups and organizations are listed for informational purposes, and listing does not imply publisher endorsement of their activities.

Library of Congress Cataloging-in-Publication Data

Bowley, Mary Frances, author.
 Make it zero : the movement to safeguard every child / Mary Frances Bowley with Jennifer Bradley Franklin.
     pages cm
 Includes bibliographical references.
 ISBN 978-0-8024-1385-7
1. Children--Services for--United States. 2. Child welfare--United States. 3. Social action--United States. I. Franklin, Jennifer Bradley, author. II. Title.
 HV741.B696 2015

 362.70973--dc23

                        2015032673

We hope you enjoy this book from Moody Publishers. Our goal is to provide high-quality, thought-provoking books and products that connect truth to your real needs and challenges. For more information on other books and products written and produced from a biblical perspective, go to www.moodypublishers.com or write to:

Moody Publishers
820 N. LaSalle Boulevard
Chicago, IL 60610

1 3 5 7 9 10 8 6 4 2

Printed in the United States of America

THIS BOOK IS DEDICATED

TO THE LEGIONS OF LEADERS

WHO ARE LOCKING ARMS

SAFEGUARDING CHILDREN

TO MAKE IT ZERO.

CONTENTS

Foreword / 11

How This Book Will Make a Difference . . . And So Can You / 15

FOREWORD

Few will have the greatness to bend history, but each of us can work to change a small portion of events . . . Each time a [person] stands up for an ideal, or acts to improve the lot of others, or strikes out against injustice, he sends forth a tiny ripple of hope and crossing each other from a million different centers of energy and daring those ripples to build a current which can sweep down the mightiest walls of oppression and resistance.
—SENATOR ROBERT F. KENNEDY

If slavery is not wrong, then nothing is wrong.
—PRESIDENT ABRAHAM LINCOLN

I'M ALWAYS AMAZED at how our stories are woven together. Especially when you learn, sometimes even years later, that a connection you made, a small act of kindness, a moment of sharing insights, has had a ripple effect that went on to change the trajectory of others' lives forever.

That's what I love most about this inspiring book *Make It Zero*. By reading it, you're going to be connected in a totally new way, your eyes opened to issues you may be geographically close to but completely removed from because you don't realize they're happening in your backyard. I can promise you they *are* affecting you, whether you know it or not.

Like most of us, I didn't start out with this awareness. I grew up in a typical middle-class family, but in college, I wanted to step outside my own set of experiences and make a difference. Right after my freshman year, I spent six months in Bogota, Colombia, working with women and children living in the *barrios*, an experience that opened my eyes. As I got to know them, I came to understand what these women already knew: there was a pandemic of child abuse keeping generations of Colombians from moving forward from extreme generational poverty. I met a little girl who had all of her front teeth knocked out by an abuser.

My heart shattered in a way it never had before. I came back to my tiny room and broke down weeping. It was the first time I remember experiencing the presence of God. I felt His loving grace and kindness, and I knew that this kind of injustice broke His father's heart to pieces. I felt Him saying, "You can be part of the solution. See how your heart breaks? Mine breaks too, and I've equipped people—like you—to do something about it." Justice is at the core of God's heart, and so it's become a driving motivation for me.

Shortly thereafter, I became a Christian and sought more ways to be involved at home. After graduation, I built a career working in the intersecting space of social justice and faith. I served as faith advisor to John Kerry in 2004 and went to work at the White House in the Office of Faith-Based and Neighborhood Partnerships, collaborating with other leaders of various faiths to make a difference.

In 2011, along with other colleagues from the White House, we were invited to attend the Passion Conference in Atlanta. Drawn to the twin causes of justice and ending human trafficking, presenters drove home the point that exploitation was happening to American children and teens. I was shocked at the atrocities going on under our noses. We took the issue straight to the president, and combating modern slavery became a focus at the highest levels of government.

It was through this White House effort that I met Brian Gallagher, president and CEO, of United Way Worldwide, who become compelled to get United Way involved in the fight to eradicate human trafficking and modern slavery. In June of 2015, I helped United Way launch its first ever anti-trafficking initiative, the United Way Center on Human Trafficking and Slavery.

As you'll see in the book, that chain of events can be traced directly back to Mary Frances's relationship with Passion. I am amazed at the way one conversation, one moment of connection, can literally pave the way for change at a global scale. I didn't know it at the time, but Mary Frances is the reason I am working to combat human trafficking today.

As you'll see on the pages here, issues are connected too. It's a bit like a funnel: Children who have been abused, those living in poverty, foster kids aging out of a broken system, and those who don't have enough to eat are easier targets for those who wish to misuse them. Exploitation is one of the worst things that can happen to a young person, but addressing the "feeder issues" greatly reduces the risk. If we're really going to change it—to become modern-day abolitionists—we have to take a comprehensive approach, as this book does. Best yet, there are simple actions you can take, outlined in crystal clarity, to move the needle toward change.

One thing I can promise you: After reading *Make It Zero*, you won't be able to look away, to turn a blind eye to what's happening all around you. If one child in America is at risk, they all are.

We have to do what we can as individuals and communities and lean on our leaders to allocate greater resources to these causes. Look at what we've done to fight malaria, AIDS, tuberculosis, and polio. What if we employed similar comprehensive efforts to eradicate the hunger, poverty, isolation, abuse and ultimately, the human trafficking of our children and youth? I know we can.

My Christian faith has become part of what drives me; it's central to who I am. But no matter what your beliefs are—you can (and should!) be part of the solution. I encourage you to read this wonderful book and decide how you will be involved. Tell your friends, family, and colleagues. Become the eyes and ears of your community. Lend your influence, your time, and your heart to be one more thread in this beautiful tapestry of change.

We are all connected, and we can all do something to help make the number of vulnerable young people in the United States zero.

—MARA VANDERSLICE KELLY
Executive director, United Way Center on Human Trafficking and Slavery

HOW THIS BOOK WILL MAKE A DIFFERENCE . . . AND SO CAN YOU

Start by doing what's necessary;
then do what's possible; and suddenly
you are doing the impossible.
—FRANCIS OF ASSISI

LOTS OF THE STORIES contained in this book will tug at your heartstrings and open your eyes to the plight of children at risk all around us.

It's not a racial or ethnic issue. It's not a poor issue or a rich one. It's not something that happens only in inner cities or just in the suburbs. It crosses all racial, socioeconomic, and geographic lines and is truly affecting our entire nation. You'll see.

You'll discover how poverty, hunger, isolation, abuse, and trafficking are endangering our children. These stories here are hopeful, every last one of them. Again, you'll see.

Becoming aware of the magnitude of these struggles may feel like trying to save the *Titanic* from sinking by shoveling out water with a teaspoon. We encourage you to resist the natural urge to become overwhelmed at the magnitude of what you'll learn. Instead, be encouraged by what you—one—and others like you—another one and one and one—who are embarking on this journey of awareness and action can do to help solve these problems. We can almost promise you won't look at the world the same way after you're touched by the true tales on these pages.

A word about truth: everything you'll read on the pages of *Make It Zero* is true. However, when it comes to those who have asked for privacy, or the circumstances of how they came to intersect our book were dire and anonymity is necessary, we've changed their names or identifying details to protect them.

My first interaction with helping to solve for such complexities was when I founded Wellspring Living, an Atlanta-based haven and home for women and girls who have been trafficked for sex. Starting in 2001, we've helped provide housing, care, intensive counseling, life skills training, and job placement for many young women. I told many of their stories—both heart-wrenching and encouraging—in *The White Umbrella*.

The work we began with Wellspring Living has given me a unique window into these beautiful lives, and as I began to understand how the circumstances of their lives have led them to a place of exploitation, I've seen a common theme emerge: most of them were vulnerable as children. It's been with this realization that I'm impressed that *when*, not *if*, we correct the factors that lead to childhood vulnerability, we can make a difference in the lives of those children and in the lives of the adults they'll grow up to be.

The issue of vulnerable children is overwhelming, to put it very mildly. The numbers alone are enough to make some throw up their hands and say, "It's too big of an issue; what can I as one person do?"

It's a multifaceted matter requiring more than a surface knowledge to truly end the heinous crimes attacking our children. But like any complex issue, it can be tackled, broken into bite-sized pieces, and systematically solved. This book is written with the intent to break down not just the issues but also offer action-oriented solutions.

Each of the five sections—Poverty, Hunger, Isolation, Abuse, and Trafficking—will close with practical Take Action ideas and stories of people who did.

Many people will tell their compelling stories in the pages of this book. Mine is not as dramatic as the others you'll read, but I'd like to tell it anyway and show how the eyes of one ordinary woman were opened, and everything changed. This is my story.

Most of us are safe and we like to stay that way within the confines of what's familiar, controllable, and easy. Most of us live our lives with preconceived ideas about people and the neighborhoods in our cities. If we drive into a neighborhood with beautiful homes and pristine yards, we believe that everyone has their life together. If we drive through a part of town where the homes are run-down and the yards are not well landscaped, we assume there is crime and violence. Innately we know that what we see on the outside is not always true, but it's very easy to not take the next step and look below the surface to find out what's really going on.

I've been a victim of this way of thinking. Often though, getting outside of ourselves creates the most memorable, defining experiences. It's certainly been that way for me.

Drawing me out of my confined world came when I met the incomparable Annette Trotter. It was 1999, and we were working together on a faith-based event. We spent hours together strategizing on how to build the audience and market this event to become multicultural and multigenerational.

Annette and I had completely different backgrounds. I grew up in a town of fewer than ten thousand, and Annette grew up in the heart of Atlanta. We found common ground because we were both kindergarten teachers, and we became fast friends as we worked together planning the upcoming event. One morning during a strategy session, Annette turned to me with her contagious laugh and said, "Girl, you need to see the real Atlanta. Do you want me to educate you?"

Since Annette had become a trusted, fun-loving friend, I was thrilled to go on any journey with her, so I quickly replied, "Yes!"

We met the next morning and as I drove, allowing Annette to guide me, she directed me through poor and underserved neighborhoods I'd never seen, down what seemed one-lane streets to a little church with white siding and peeling paint.

We met Winnifred Benson, a nurse who had laid aside her career to serve alongside her husband, the assistant pastor of Southwest Christian Church. I listened with amazement as Winnie described her Mother's Morning Out program, where she taught young moms skills for caring for themselves and their children. It was the Thursday before Memorial Day and the summer sun was becoming unbearable, so we followed Winnie to her home. Standing on her porch, Winnie pointed out home after home and told what was happening inside these run-down houses. She described how she ensured that every child got the food and clothing needed. The stories of desperation and need were overwhelming, but nothing stopped this one-woman force from doing what she could.

> **I realized that my dull world of doing life with people just like me had to be diversified; my circle of friends and influencers must be expanded.**

By the time we left the neighborhood, my perspective had changed. My life was marked forever. I would never drive through a marginalized community again and assume that only bad things were happening. I would never look at our city in the same way. I would never think that the little things I did for my friends were enough. In fact, I was sure that my circle of friends was about to change and widen dramatically.

Because of that day, I realized that my dull world of doing life with people just like me had to be diversified; my circle of friends and influencers must be expanded. The new relationships I was forming were already bringing a flavor and richness to my life that was indescribable. I realized we didn't have to be alike to be great friends. My heart was full.

Each of us is only one person, but one person motivated for change is powerful. And one person who brings two or three or four (or more?) equally passionate, motivated friends along for the ride has the potential to create a movement, a groundswell, to effect change.

What if we all looked at children through the eyes of their potential? What if we helped our circle of influence to grasp this concept? What if we help our children to gain compassion and understanding for those who are not like themselves? Could we make the world safer for our children and others?

Get ready to be changed and to be a part of this groundswell that can change the world for the better. You can be part of making the world a safer place for our nation's children. Together we can change these overwhelming numbers to the sweetest one of all, *ZERO.* Together we can change the overwhelming number of children at risk and: Make It Zero.

Can we? I believe we can!

—MARY FRANCES BOWLEY

make it
zero

In 2013, 46.6 million people lived in poverty in America and a third of these individuals were children under the age of eighteen.[1]

In 2013, 31 percent of America's children (23,101,000) had parents who lacked secure employment.[2]

In 2013, 1,404,000 (8 percent) of America's teens were not in school and not employed.[3]

PART ONE

ZERO POVERTY

If a family's total income is less than the dollar value of the appropriate threshold, then that family and every individual in it are considered to be in poverty. Similarly, if an unrelated individual's total income is less than the appropriate threshold, then that individual is considered to be in poverty. The poverty thresholds do not vary geographically, but they are updated for inflation and using the Consumer Price Index.

ONE LIFELINE

Overcoming poverty is not a task of charity,
it is an act of justice.
—NELSON MANDELA

I LOVE A GREAT STORY, don't you? Of course, it's wonderful if it's a tale of singular heroism and valor, but I've found that sometimes it's even better when it's an epic tale that involves several stories woven together like a tapestry, the thread of connection only clear after the fact. That's the way this one happened.

I knew that if our Wellspring Living graduates and those coming through the Empowered Living Academy, i.e., women who had survived trafficking and/or who were teetering on the edge of great risk, couldn't find sustainable, living-wage career employment after having completed intensive life skills training and counseling, then they might soon find themselves back in a tragic situation. It broke our hearts to think that those who had made so much progress could slip back into allowing someone else to control their destinies again or giving away their power to make their own choices.

When I think of Hire Hope and the way it all came together, I'm convinced that if just one of the key people in the story had ignored the tug on their heartstrings, it wouldn't exist. In fact, little did I know that one of the key players felt a call on her life long before she intersected with me.

When I met Amy Henderson, it was easy to think that the beautiful blonde with crystal clear eyes flecked with green and blue had lived something of a charmed life. What I soon learned was that her heart had been broken in so many ways that her life's story was just a bit tough enough to give her a unique window into the lives and hearts of our women at Wellspring. You see, Amy had experienced true pain, true rejection, and true vulnerability. So I'd like to introduce you to Amy herself and let her tell you her story. Trust me: it's a really good one!

Amy's Story:

I grew up in a normal-looking, all-American family in the northern suburbs of Atlanta, the second of four siblings, with parents who were still married, which seemed a rarity among my peers. From the outside looking in, life was good and it looked like we were living the dream. But when you peeled back the layers, you saw a lot of pain.

While we lived in a relatively affluent area, we struggled intensely to make ends meet. Both my parents were in and out of jobs, so it always felt like we were one financial emergency away from disaster. While my parents did the best they knew how, they couldn't shield us from the strain financial struggles bring. All my siblings and I faced intense anxiety over how we would be taken care of, have food to eat, have reliable transportation to and from school, and such. Would the lights be turned off yet again? The scariest part wasn't going without, it was anticipating the ensuing arguments we'd lie awake listening to, after our parents thought we were asleep.

My mother struggled with the highs and lows that come with mental illness, and as a result, my life was full of uncertainty and often felt like one big, death-defying emotional roller coaster. Her depression led her to dark places that ultimately landed her in and out of jail and eventually prison for financial reasons while she was trying to help our family escape bankruptcy.

My entire world was rocked. I was in high school and like so many teens, desperate to cover up the turmoil at home by making things look "normal." Some of my closest friends didn't even know that Mom was incarcerated. Trying to pick up the financial slack, my dad retreated into his work and was rarely home. To call this "trauma" seems like a gross understatement. Since my older sister was away at college, I tried to care for my younger siblings and provide some of the stability I lacked. It was entirely too much for my still-developing high school self to bear.

Fast-forward to college: I went to a big, Southern university one state over and began to see some very real cracks in my identity. The pain I worked so hard to hide began to slowly seep out. I vacillated between trying to maintain a perfect image and acting out with all sorts of desperate behavior. I used relationships to validate my broken identity, with no idea how to honor myself. Honestly, I didn't know if there was anything in me worth honoring. I spiraled out of control with breakup after breakup, hoping to find a relationship that would validate me and allow me to feel protected. As you can imagine, it was a fruitless pursuit that yielded nothing but deeper devastation.

"Your life is so perfect. How could you possibly relate to me?"

Soon after college, the tide seemed to turn. I met and fell in love with someone I believed would be the perfect man to help me put the finishing touches on the portrait of perfection I desperately wanted. He was everything I had ever dreamed of. He wore his faith on his sleeve, he was Southern, athletic, smart, and model-good-looking. At just twenty-three, he pursued me well, with the kind of respect I always knew was right. Without a dime to our names, we married quickly, and while not perfect, we spent the first year in what I wholeheartedly believed was wedded bliss. I had fallen so deeply in love with this man, for everything he was and honestly, for all the things he wasn't. What I did know was that he was my very best friend and I was his. I had loved prior to him, but no one had stolen my heart as he did. I finally felt like I'd found my safe place.

In the early months of marriage, one of my best friends (who had been a bridesmaid in my wedding) deliberately fell out of touch. After six months of her not returning phone calls, I finally reached her and she agreed to meet. Over coffee I asked why she'd become so distant, and she replied, "Amy, your life is so perfect. How could you possibly relate to me?" And considering the childhood family secrets I still kept purposefully tucked away, she was disturbingly right. I had worked hard to cover up the pain with the perfect shades of paint, putting the finishing touches on my attempt at perfection. I was happily married, had a great job and a cute home on the outskirts of Atlanta. What more could a young woman ask, right?

That dream was shattered when my husband came home one day and told me that he had never loved me and was leaving. Over the next few months, I uncovered some of the worst kinds of emotional betrayal within a marriage, the kinds that can shatter a wife's confidence and wound in places that last. Here it is again, I thought, trying to manage the panic rising up inside of me. This is what trauma really feels like.

I grieved the end of my marriage intensely. I still loved my husband so much and felt like my life had turned into a bad dream from which I hoped to one day wake up. My recent conversation with that friend rang in my ears, and I thought, "No one will ever say that my life is too perfect or charmed again."

Yet through it all, I had a sense through my faith in God that this particular part of my story would really be used in some bigger way. I heard God say, "Grieve this trauma well, because I'm going to use it to accomplish something you can't even imagine."

In the aftermath of my divorce, I lost my job and found myself facing financial battles that felt all too familiar. When I finally landed a new job at Randstad, a national staffing and recruiting firm, I had a huge heart for and interest in the vulnerable and unemployed, particularly young women at risk as I essentially had been.

In the spring of 2013, I was invited to attend a vision lunch. A group of twenty women met at an idyllic farm and, seated around a huge wooden table piled with Southern food, Mary Frances spoke. "How can we live in the heart of the South—the Bible Belt—and be such a huge hub of human trafficking and the atrocities that go with it?" one woman asked.

I was intrigued. That day was the introduction to my heart breaking for these women.

I kept seeking ways to be involved with the issue, something "big" as I felt I'd heard God promising me, but nothing seemed to be happening. *Did I hear wrong?* I wondered. I felt almost embarrassed to tell people my dream of making a difference, because it seemed that my life, though I'd continued to thrive and be promoted at my job, had stalled out.

Meanwhile, I made a new friend, Chandelle Fairley, who had moved back to town to manage another Atlanta branch of Randstad. We bonded over holding similar positions within the company, and in an effort to help her meet others in town, I invited her to volunteer with me at the Passion conference in January 2014. [You can read the inspiring story of Passion later in the book at "One Spark Can Set the World on Fire."] That year, one of the big focuses of the gathering of twenty thousand college students was ending human trafficking around the world. As Chandelle and I leaned against the doors of Philips Arena (we were door holders and greeters), we turned to each other in the dark and said, "This year, we're going to do something tangible about this issue." How could we know that these horrors were happening in our own city and not do something? Again, I felt a little ridiculous voicing my interest in the issue with no defined plan, but I still felt so stirred up about it that I couldn't help myself.

The very next Monday, I got a call from Chandelle asking if I could represent her in the office for an impromptu meeting that Thursday. You could have knocked me over with a feather. The meeting would include Mary Frances, whom I'd heard speak more than a year before, Gemma Filliben, an executive with Randstad, and Tom Miller, the then-CIO of Coca-Cola.

Little did I know that Mary Frances and her team had been working on a new initiative called Empowered Living Academy and they were wrestling with the issue of helping at-risk women find sustainable, career-oriented employment. She gave a local TED talk about the issue. Tom saw it and forwarded it to just about every influential person he knew, including Gemma, who was high ranking at Randstad. She was flying to Atlanta, and we were going to meet to see how my company could be involved. Chandelle would be traveling for work and therefore unavailable, so I was the one asked to represent Atlanta Randstad offices and host the meeting.

At 7:30 in the morning, we all gathered in a ninth-floor conference room with the sun rising behind the glass windows. I listened as Mary Frances spoke about the barriers to this population of women finding employment beyond working in strip clubs, at low-paying fast-food restaurants, and/or in minimum wage retail. The idea behind the meeting was that perhaps Randstad could supply professional women to mentor those ladies who were on the career readiness track in the Empowered Living Academy.

I heard myself blurting out, "We can do way more than mentor them. We can find them jobs!" After all, we were one of the world's largest staffing agencies. I felt three pairs of widened eyes turn to me. It was unanimous: we were going to figure out a way to do it.

Looking back, I still can't believe how it all came together and turned into something far bigger than any one individual. Chandelle and I began downloading curriculum from the Internet, spending our after-work hours researching activities and exercises we could do with the participants to help shepherd them on their way to a real career that could support not only themselves, but their families as well.

As we prepared to launch the still-unnamed program, we met with the first seven women in a conference room on loan at Coca-Cola. The nervous, excited energy was palpable. We went around the table and introduced ourselves, sharing just a bit about our lives. When it was my turn, I found my story tumbling out—the trauma of my family's financial struggles and Mom's prison time, my divorce, the tailspin that followed, and the struggle in the aftermath to land on my feet financially and careerwise.

It was a pretty unbelievable moment: I felt an instant connection with each of them as, in their eyes, I went from someone who might look like an authoritative professional with my corporate position and the clothes that went with it to someone they could relate to. No, I hadn't lived through the horrors of being on the streets, but one tragic twist or turn in my life and my story could have looked a lot more like theirs. A flood of gratefulness washed over me for the path that I'd walked, through all of the hard moments—yes, and trauma—I'd experienced and for the opportunity for a window and connection with these young women, each of whom had so much potential.

We launched our program the end of February, just six weeks after Chandelle and I stood in that darkened stadium, promising to be involved in this issue. We determined we would start with seven weeks of classroom work. The women were already doing their Empowered Living Academy curriculum Monday through Thursday, and on Fridays they spent the day at Randstad, learning about office etiquette, scheduling meetings, social media skills, business writing, and more. Then, the next step was to give them a paid apprenticeship within Randstad for ten weeks. During these two and a half months, the women's pay was commensurate with an entry-level office job, i.e., well above minimum wage, and they had the opportunity to gain experience that would be a true resume builder. Finally, each of the women would be placed in a career-track job.

We were thrilled with the progress of the first "class" and had a small ceremony to commemorate their accomplishments, following the apprentice-ship. One executive caught wind of it and alerted Linda Galipeau, CEO of all of Randstad, North America about what we were up to. She asked us to prepare a presentation and share our vision and plan. To say we were nervous is an enormous understatement. Linda is accomplished, decisive, and powerful.

Chandelle, Gemma, and I laid out our ideas for training and getting these young women jobs. Linda listened stoically, nodding some, pointing to a slide and asking a question, here and there. Then, silence.

We all held our breath, knowing she had the power to kill the program with one word.

Instead, she smiled and said, "You had me at *hello*." We let out the air we'd been holding, breathed a collective sigh of relief and, to our astonishment, she went on to say that she wanted to put resources behind our simple ragtag program to formalize it, create a logo and a name that would resonate, help with any legal obstacles to getting these women sustainable employment, and help with marketing. That was how Hire Hope was officially born.

Since then, we've placed our graduates in positions within Randstad, with Coca-Cola and other Fortune 500 companies, and they're thriving in jobs in diversity and inclusion departments, IT and data fields, and administrative roles.

Our pilot program has been repeated, refined, and replicated, so that now we're having an even larger quarterly class of women come through Hire Hope. Our plan is to continue refining it in Atlanta and then to look for cities with high at-risk populations for trafficking that also have a strong Randstad presence, so this creative and groundbreaking approach can touch even more communities around the United States.

We meet them where they are, hold their hands and say, "Kick hard! Look—swim like this! Keep breathing; you're almost there."

The "getting them a job" part is central, of course, but the program is so much more than that. It provides someone to believe in and with these women, so that they can see that there's a hope and a future full of possibilities. When someone is in the depths of poverty, there is often a pileup of defeat over time; hopeless days have turned into months, months into years, and perhaps even generations, during which defeat becomes familiar. The hope of something more, well, who has time for that when you're just trying to survive?

I liken it to someone who's drifted off at sea, not knowing how it happened, and once she realizes and starts trying to fight, the undertow sweeps her out even farther. As time passes, she loses sight of the shore and, treading water as hard as possible, becomes exhausted. After all, people weren't made for the open sea, with its merciless waves. The shore becomes a hope that seems far too grand to dream of ever seeing again. They may think they need a life preserver, but while a life preserver is good for the immediate need of not drowning, it won't guide them to dry land. What that castaway needs is someone to swim out, through the choppy water, with a reminder that dry land is a vigorous swim away. But it's possible to make it!

That's what Hire Hope is to these women. We meet them where they are, hold their hands and say, "Kick hard! Look—swim like this! Keep breathing; you're almost there." And, once they reach the shore, we help them revive the notion of a flourishing life and career that will take them places they've previously never dared to hope.

Looking back, I can only see my whole story as beautiful. Yes, there's been tremendous pain, but I love how it's being used to make a difference. At the heart of it, my story bears similarities to our Hire Hope participants'; there's been trauma, yes, but there is redemption and the heartbreak has given way to new growth and beauty. For me, I wouldn't change a thing.

REACT

What do you think of Randstad's approach? Have you benefitted from a mentor in a work situation? Are you a business owner or in another position of being able to train another person in office etiquette, scheduling, business writing, social media, and so on?

CHAPTER 2

THE ONES ADD UP

Never doubt that a small group of thoughtful,
committed citizens can change the world . . .
—MARGARET MEAD

IT IS MY BELIEF that disrupting the cycle of poverty can only truly happen as young moms find access to opportunity to secure living wage employment.

One area we struggled with was assisting young women in finding sustainable employment. We knew that if we could address this issue, we could help effect a generational shift—moms who could provide for their families meant a new generation of little ones wouldn't be as vulnerable to risk of abandonment and isolation. No matter what creative solutions we explored, we seemed to hit roadblocks at every turn.

For years, I thought just our organization experienced this problem, but the more I spoke to those who work with this age group in social services, the more I realized that this is a widespread issue.

And the more I realized how a chain of "ones" working together can work on solutions.

LAURA

Laura Clark, a member of Wellspring's board, took it on herself to do extensive research on this problem. She reported, "I believe we need a program with these goals: self-awareness, skills and interest discovery, resume writing, interview skills, career matching, and professional dress." Then she added, "It would be wonderful to have a corporation who would offer paid internships to help these young women build a resume."

TOM

In 2012 at a conference on trafficking, I met Tom Miller, then-CIO of Coke Enterprises, and we stayed in touch, later meeting back in Atlanta to discuss the needs for fighting this problem on the home front. We didn't come up with anything specific Tom could do immediately, but we touched base often over the next eighteen months, since his heart was captured by the issue of trafficking right in his company's hometown of Atlanta.

One morning Tom called and enthusiastically told me, "I think I know a way I can help Wellspring Living. I shared your TED Talk with a lot of influential, connected people." Little did I know that his forwarded email video clip was the lynchpin that connected me to the next one who would help take this from a problem to a solution. One of the recipients of Tom's email blitz was Randstad's Gemma Filliben, whose involvement you read about in Amy's story.

GEMMA

Shortly after receiving my video, in which I laid out a case for creating a generational shift of employment, Gemma called me. She explained how her employer, Randstad, is one of the largest staffing agencies in the world and she believed that they could help Wellspring Living create a pathway for employment for the women we serve.

AMY AND CHANDELLE

Within weeks of meeting by phone, Gemma came to Atlanta and met with Laura, Tom, and me. She asked two Atlanta Randstad staffers, Amy and Chandelle, to accelerate this process.

That morning we met, and Laura explained what she believed were vital elements in helping young women move toward a path of sustainable employment and self-sufficiency for themselves and sometimes their young families. Gemma listened and quietly said, "We already have that program."

She went on to say that Randstad created a program called Explore Work for high school seniors and she felt certain that we could get permission to use the curriculum with the women coming through the Wellspring Living program. Gemma agreed to send the electronic version of the curriculum to Laura and encouraged us to make it practical for the young women we serve. Within days, Laura edited the book, talking extensively with Gemma, Amy, and Chandelle along the way.

THE TEAM OF ONES

Just two weeks later, Laura, Gemma, Chandelle, Amy, and I met with our long-range planning team to share our vision of what the program could look like. Soon after that we met with seven young women from Wellspring Living to introduce them to this new venture. We didn't have a name or all the details figured out, nor could we know what the outcome would be, but we rolled ahead with great anticipation.

Each week, I watched these precious women come alive as they learned about professional dress, office etiquette, and the practical use of computer software. They began to know themselves and believe they could have big dreams for their lives. I'll never forget the morning I joined one of the training sessions and saw women who previously had seemed only cautiously hopeful now light up when they described all they'd discovered about themselves and shared their plan of action for the future.

Four weeks into the training, Randstad decided they would offer a paid apprenticeship to each of the women as a reinforcement and practice of what they'd learned and to build their resumes. During the apprenticeship, each one embraced her new opportunity so well that their managers wanted them to join their staff. So by the end of the summer, each woman was offered employment on a more permanent basis.

Each week, we solidified our resolve to make a path for young women to secure sustainable employment. We knew this was such a win for the women of Wellspring Living. That was great, but many others needed this opportunity. We couldn't keep it to ourselves.

DAVE AND BILLY AND BEYOND

We began exploring how we could deliver these services to women outside of our residential programming. We had been looking for a facility we could purchase or rent, but found no real options. Dave Abrahamson, our board chair, was intimately engaged in these conversations. In an unrelated meeting with Billy Holley, the CFO of YMCA of Metro Atlanta, Dave asked if they had empty classrooms that we could use to do programming. Billy said yes.

This yes led us on a path to working out how YMCA of Metro Atlanta and Wellspring Living could partner. We strategized and dreamed of a day we could offer what we believed was a pioneering effort. In the fall of 2014, Wellspring Living officially launched the Empowered Living Academy at the Carver YMCA in downtown Atlanta, inviting forty-nine other nonprofits and agencies to refer young women into this "mini technical/therapeutic school." It seemed the perfect way to grow beyond just Wellspring Living, since there are so many dynamic organizations doing good work with young women in need.

Beginning this community-based program was new for us. We wondered if the young women who enrolled would consistently attend and complete what this ten-week opportunity required. We had many questions, but we were committed. One of the most satisfying developments was that each woman who began in October was still tracking with the program in December when we hosted a completion celebration.

At first we thought this could have been just a onetime achievement, but we soon learned that the young women enrolling in the program were serious about moving from hopelessness toward a brighter future.

ONE EAGER PARTICIPANT

While all of the women in the Empowered Living Academy have compelling stories, Brandi Gossett embodies the sheer determination and tenacity they have to have. Brandi grew up in Rome, Georgia, without a lot of things the average American girl enjoys. Her mom was a single parent who had to work multiple jobs just to pay the bills.

Brandi was the oldest, so she took care of her little sister, starting in fourth grade. After she graduated high school, Brandi met up with some girlfriends who were making great money, more than

Brandi could fathom. They told her she could help her mom even more if she would join them and work in a strip club. What happened after that encounter was quite a journey to the place Brandi was when we sat down to talk. I was intrigued by her story, her fortitude and willpower! She definitely has a story to tell, and I believe she will inspire you as she has inspired me.

Brandi's Story:

I just wanted to earn money, go home, and not let this culture suck me in. That's what I did for three years. Even though I was determined not to let the club get to me, it did. I was so tired of the hours and stress all around me.

I wasn't really looking for a way out. I thought this is just what I have to do. I have no other options. Victoria's Friends [to learn about this outstanding organization, visit victoriasfriends.com] came by the club often, but I never really connected with them. I remember around Easter, they brought Easter baskets. I thought that was so kind, but I just didn't think I needed their help.

I had never felt threatened or afraid because I kept my guard up, but one evening, everything changed. I had just broken up with my boyfriend and I was teary-eyed as I left work. It had been a long day and I had to park pretty far away from the club. As I walked the long trek to my car, I felt like someone was following me. I reached my car and drove to my apartment. I thought I'd lost whoever was stalking me, but as I parked, it looked like another car pulled in. I ran to my apartment as fast as I could. The guy was right on my heels. I pushed my key into the lock and opened the door, but I wasn't fast enough. He came in right behind me and began to hit me; he raped me and afterwards wouldn't leave. I struggled so hard to get away, but he kept pursuing me. I finally escaped to my bedroom and locked the door. I didn't know how long I would have before he would break the door down. I called 911, but I didn't think anyone could get there in time. I really thought he would kill me, and I remember praying, "God, if you will get me out of this, I will do something different with my life." In just a few minutes, the noises outside my door stopped. A few minutes later, the police arrived. I reported everything and went to the hospital, where they did a forensic interview and rape kit. I still wondered if they would ever find him, and if he would come back after me.

I didn't forget that promise I made to God, and then I remembered the Easter baskets from Victoria's Friends and found Victoria Teague's card. I called Victoria, and she was incredible. I had such a hard time talking about what happened to me. Victoria listened to me, comforted me, and helped me get a different job, this one in a restaurant. The money wasn't nearly as good, but at least my body wasn't on offer.

I'm going to do whatever I have to do to take advantage of this opportunity.

Victoria stayed right by me over the next four years. She encouraged me during my pregnancy and the birth of my daughter. She was with me when my rapist went to trial. Yes, the police found the man and discovered that he had brutally raped two other women before me. With Victoria's support and direction, I was able to testify and see him go away for life plus twenty years. I can't say enough about Victoria's consistent care. She was always checking in on me.

Victoria knew that I wanted to do more with my life than work in a restaurant, but because of my work history and skill level, it was about the only thing I could do. When Victoria heard about the Empowered Living Academy, she called. Even though I lived over eighty miles away, I told Victoria that I absolutely wanted to enroll. I remember meeting Alice, the intake coordinator, and interviewing for the academy. She asked me if I could commit to traveling over a hundred and fifty miles, five days a week for ten weeks. I told her, "I have nothing to lose. I don't care if I have to slide down icy roads; I'm going to do whatever I have to do to take advantage of this opportunity. I have to do this for my daughter."

So early each morning, I'd get my daughter ready and together we'd begin the trek to the south side of Atlanta. I'm so glad I did. I learned so much about myself through the group sessions and employment classes and so much that prepared me for the professional environment; I received a ton of support. I'm now in my apprenticeship with Randstad in my hometown, and I'm looking forward to becoming a full-time employee soon.

As Brandi and I reflected on her incredible journey, she said, beaming, "I remember dreaming about the things I do right now. My job with Randstad is amazing! I get to help others find employment. I really feel important, and that I'm helping make a change in people's lives. I never thought four years ago I would be where I am today!"

REACT

Does it surprise you that someone with Brandi's background could experience such a turnaround? How did the simple act of bringing Easter baskets to this club trigger a life change? What other simple acts can lead to surprising changes?

CHAPTER 3

ONE SOCIAL WORKER, TWO FRIENDS

Do your little bit of good where you are. It's those little bits of good put together that overwhelm the world.
—DESMOND TUTU

HAS ANYONE EVER been radically generous to you? I know, in my own life, I can look back and see gifts, second chances (or third or fourth ones), and turns of events that were completely beyond my control, but redirected the course of my life's events for the better. For some of us, these moments were small, fleeting incidences that have elicited a heartfelt "thank you" and not much more. But for others, like the story you're about to read, the generosity is so overwhelming that it changes the very course of an entire existence, opening up possibilities that weren't possible before.

Tanetta lost her dad at the tender age of seven. She was the apple of his eye, and he was the primary source of her stability and safety. Though her mom had the best of intentions to raise her little girl well, she also had a huge drug problem and was rarely around, plagued by her own demons and troubles. Tanetta was sent to live with her grandmother and was lucky if she saw her mother even one weekend a month. By the time she was seventeen, her grandmother had died, and Tanetta spent the next five years of her life bouncing from one family member to another.

During this time her mother's health was failing from years of hard drugs, so Tanetta started skipping school to help her. Without any stability, she made some unwise, but not surprising choices and found herself pregnant with twins. Her baby girls, Jasmin and Joelle, were born when Tanetta was just twenty, not yet a bona fide adult herself, and life was completely overwhelming. It is no wonder that she failed her test to graduate from high school. Studying wasn't a priority when more urgent things like getting diapers, obtaining food, and trying to sleep when she could were the basics she needed to survive. Seeking comfort where she could find it, in less than a year, Tanetta found herself pregnant again. Jackson was born sixteen months after her twin girls. To say that life was extremely difficult is an understatement, but Tanetta loved her children and resolved to do everything she could to provide for them and give them a better life. That goal was off to a slow start, since she couldn't find a job while living with family and getting only enough government assistance to squeak by.

> **She thought, *There's no way I can do that. Doesn't she see how much I've got on my plate already?***

ONE WHO NOTICED

One balmy September afternoon, Tanetta was walking toward home with her three children in tow (quite the entourage for this young mother, as you can imagine!) when she caught the attention of Division of Family and Children's Services (DFCS) worker Marjorie Bell, who lived in the neighborhood.

Marjorie is only a few years older than Tanetta, with jet-black hair, kind brown eyes, and a ready smile. Even though Marjorie had never met Tanetta before, she was determined to do something to help. So she stopped and struck up a conversation. Tanetta responded in her usual, open way as Marjorie told her that she needed to check out Wellspring Living's new Empowered Living Academy. Tanetta listened patiently, but thought, *There's no way I can do that. Doesn't she see how much I've got on my plate already?*

Marjorie got to know Tanetta a bit more over the coming weeks and was so insistent that she actually filled out the application for her. For every obstacle Tanetta brought up, she found that Empowered Living Academy made provisions, including public transit passes and childcare. Tanetta was accepted to the program and Marjorie made sure she arrived at orientation, where she learned more about the opportunities she would be afforded there. Tanetta began the Academy's curriculum in October of 2014 to obtain her GED (the high school equivalency test), and hoped one day to enter the career readiness track so that she could make strides to seriously improving the outlook for her little family.

Marjorie was the first compassionate woman who set Tanetta on a journey down a different path. But it wasn't long after Tanetta enrolled in the Academy that she met two other caring women who would further radically impact the course of her life. While I had heard bits and pieces over the months, I knew it was *such* a good story, so I asked Tanetta and her two life-changing friends to join me for dinner to tell the whole tale and fit all of the pieces together.

TWO CAN SHARE THE LOAD

Karen Kelley and Sherri Radley work together in a state government office, and over lunch one day, Karen shared how much she cared about single moms, since she herself had been a single mom with preschoolers. As a result, she had an extra dose of compassion for them, knowing firsthand how challenging it is to do even the most basic things without anyone to help share the load. Karen went on to say that when she lived in Miami, she kept on the lookout for single moms who might need her help. Sherri listened as Karen described how she would drive by a bus stop and see a mom alone with children and offer a ride to whatever destination she needed. "I just hated to see a mother trying to get her children on a bus, sometimes struggling with strollers and diaper bags," Karen said. "In fact, I wish I could do that more here in Atlanta, but I just don't see this situation as much here."

Not even a week after that meaningful conversation, Karen came bounding into work, enthusiasm flooding her voice as she told Sherri, "Just this morning, I found a mom who needed help!" She went on to describe how, when driving a different route to the office, she passed a young mother waiting at a bus stop, with three tiny children. Of course, it was Tanetta and her sweet little ones. Karen's teenage son hopped out of the car, and asked Tanetta if his mom could take her and her children wherever she needed to go.

Tanetta told me later, "The minute I saw Karen's kind eyes, I just knew we would be safe, so I said yes and we were off to the Empowered Living Academy in downtown Atlanta. Just that one day, it saved me forty-five minutes and a ton of stress."

Karen piped in to say, "I couldn't wait to get to work and tell Sherri about my morning drive!"

As she talked to Tanetta over the next few days, Karen realized that her schedule would allow her time to provide transportation every day for Tanetta and her children. Immediately, she and Sherri got busy finding car seats and creating a plan to support this young mom. Each morning and afternoon, Tanetta told Karen about what she was learning at the Academy, from life skills to budgeting to the educational tools she needed to get her high school diploma. Karen was intrigued and noticed dramatic changes in Tanetta over the course of weeks and months.

"I watched her change from a scared mom with lots of questions and little confidence to a determined young woman. And besides the changes in Tanetta, God was speaking to my heart," Karen explained. "He knew I needed Tanetta in my life. The time in my car was more than a taxi ride, it met a need in my life that I didn't even know I had. Tanetta was becoming like a daughter to me. She was becoming a part of my family."

Tanetta was also experiencing something words couldn't describe. Tanetta smiled and looked at Karen and told me, "I've never really had a mom, you know, one who was there for me and really cared. Karen has become my mom. She checks on me every day, even on the weekends. She really cares! I never really had the love of a mom. I want to be her daughter. I love it!"

> **"I never really had the love of a mom. I want to be her daughter. I love it!"**

Over the next nine weeks, the two of them saw miracles. "I couldn't believe it the day I picked up Tanetta, and she told me that she had received a letter from the state accepting the work she had completed, granting her the high school diploma she'd been working so hard toward. I thought, *Tanetta's dream of becoming an independent woman able to care well for her children seemed to appear to be a possibility.*

Every morning, Karen checked in with her friend Sherri, updating her on Tanetta's accelerating progress. Karen loved being a part of Tanetta's life, and Sherri began to want to be involved with Tanetta as well. In January, Tanetta began the career readiness track of the Empowered Living Academy, and Karen realized she would soon need her own transportation to continue moving toward her goals. She shared this desire with her friend Sherri, but couldn't figure out how to find the money or have access to a vehicle. Sherri told me, "What Karen didn't know was that I was planning on purchasing a new car in April. The more I heard about Tanetta and her need, I knew God was nudging my heart. I knew I was supposed to give my five-year-old SUV to Tanetta and get a new car a few months earlier than planned."

"When Sherri told me of her idea, I fell into a puddle of tears!" Karen exclaimed. "What an answer to prayer. Now we just had to come up with a plan."

These two caring women shared their strategy to ask Tanetta what kind of a car she might need and how much money she might need to secure transportation. They giggled as they recounted their planning of the grand surprise.

"What an answer to prayer. Now we just had to come up with a plan!"

On the last Saturday in January, Karen picked up Tanetta, telling her she wanted to take her to meet Sherri. When they arrived, Sherri asked Tanetta if the green Mazda Tribute in her driveway would meet her needs to transport her and her three little ones. Tanetta said, "Yes, it would." Sherri encouraged Tanetta to take the car on a drive around the neighborhood. As Tanetta backed the car out of the driveway, she thought, *This is great, but there is no way I can afford this car. What am I doing here?*

When Tanetta got out of the car, Sherri put her arm around her and walked her around the car. Together, they looked at the engine, the trunk space, and confirmed that the backseat would be adequate for three car seats. Again, Sherri asked, "Tanetta, do you think this car could work for you?"

Tanetta said, "Yes, it definitely would."

Sherri then said, "Well, Tanetta, you'd better keep those keys!"

Tanetta ran over and gave Sherri a bear hug and began to weep tears of joy. In fact, they all were overcome with emotion. As they all described the experience and I watched the video Karen had taken on her phone, I was too!

ONE REDIRECTED LIFE

Receiving a car was great motivation for Tanetta to complete her career readiness classes with enthusiasm, looking forward to her apprenticeship. Tanetta's apprenticeship involved learning the industry by completing administrative tasks, creating Excel spreadsheets and tables, and observing all the aspects of the work of Randstad. Tanetta then moved into the area of talent recruitment, where she has excelled.

Recently, in a phone conversation, Tanetta expressed her disbelief at how her life has dramatically changed. Within weeks of working at the branch, her managers noticed the work ethic of this amazing young woman and asked Tanetta if she would be interested in coming on full-time with them once her apprenticeship is complete. Tanetta, like the other women in their apprenticeships, embraced this opportunity with great determination and fervor. The future is looking so different from her past, not only for Tanetta, but also for Jasmin, Joelle, and Jackson.

What a joy it is to discover even more compassionate people who want to help young women move forward with courage and create concrete provisions so they will have the confidence and the tools with which to succeed. Tanetta's story is certainly a shining example of urgent needs and providential provision through the Academy and through three compassionate women.

REACT

How did helping Tanetta with a few everyday things make a big difference? What did it mean for Tanetta to find a new "mom"?

CHAPTER 4

ONE GENERATIONAL SHIFT

*Two nations, between whom there is no intercourse
and no sympathy, who are as ignorant of each
other's habits, thoughts, and feelings, as if they were
. . . inhabitants of different planets.*
—BENJAMIN DISRAELI

"WHAT DO YOU THINK OF when I say 'the homeless'?" professor Donna Beegle asks a packed room of upperclassmen at Portland State University, writing the title in plump white letters on the board. She's impeccably dressed in tailored black pants and an amethyst jacket, with soft, straight honey-blonde hair, and it's clear from her warm and open interaction with her students that they respect her.

One young woman in jeans and a sorority T-shirt responds, "They're lazy?" asking as though her answer is a question. Another guy on the back row says, "Yeah, they're probably drug-addicted or even have a rap sheet." A chorus of agreement reverberates through the small room filled with rows of desks.

Beegle nods, giving nothing away, taking it all in. After all, she's not surprised by the responses. Next, she writes another phrase to the right of her first one. "Now what do you think of when I say 'homeless person'?" she asks quietly. The thoughtful silence that followed was broken when a young African-American man in the front row raises his hand and says, "They're probably down on their luck or maybe even could have lost a job recently. Maybe they couldn't make rent, you know?" The same woman who originally thought perhaps they were simply lazy says, "I bet they're hungry. What if they have little kids they're trying to support?" Again, heads nod, considering the realities of a *person* in a dire situation.

"Do you see what happens when we take the human element out of it? The words are not so different: 'THE homeless' versus 'a homeless PERSON,' but how we think of them changes dramatically. We need to open our minds and shift our thinking," Beegle explains, acquainting these young adults with a reality they've never known personally and never considered. It's one that she understands intimately.

It's hard to imagine Donna Beegle, PhD, as anything other than the strong, confident, articulate woman she is now. She's someone who has studied poverty extensively, but more than that, she's lived it. She speaks with such authority, passion, and deep feeling that her story should only be told from her own lips.

Donna's Story:

I was born into a family of migrant labor workers, who were themselves the children of migrant labor workers. There were so many generations of poverty that I'm not sure if there's anyone in my family tree who hasn't been among the poorest of the poor.

We would all work during the day to get food for that night.

I was born in Arizona in 1961, the fifth of six children and the only girl. I'm the only one of my siblings who hasn't done time in jail or prison. Growing up, I assumed that illiteracy, evictions, hunger, and moving frequently were normal. How would I have known any different? Everyone I knew worked hard doing whatever jobs they could get—picking strawberries or cherries or tomatoes and working temporary factory jobs.

All seven of us lived in a car.

I learned things that, while useful at the time, I now know children should never have to learn. For instance, I knew the protocol for visiting a relative in prison (bring ID, leave toys and any metal objects at home) and how to pass glasses around to get homework done, even if they weren't prescribed to me. I knew how to fix a broken tooth with superglue and how to collect moss from the woods, bundle it up, and sell it to a local plant shop so we'd be able to have a scant dinner that night. I knew my mom would go hungry if it meant I could have something to eat. These are the things that helped us survive what felt like living in a war-torn country.

We moved from Arizona to Washington to

California and finally, to Oregon. I lived in seventeen houses in twenty years. At one place in Portland, my brothers slept in a U-Haul trailer outside, while my parents and I slept where we could in a one-room shack that should have been condemned years before we rented it. The lights were shut off first and then the water, due to unpaid bills. When the bright red eviction notice appeared on our door, as they always did eventually, all seven of us lived in a car. I don't have any family photos because once, when our few belongings were in storage, a bill was left unpaid and everything was auctioned off.

Each time we moved, we had to re-learn how to access the resources in our new town. We needed to connect with churches for boxes of food and hand-me-down clothes, welfare agencies for a check to (we hoped) help us squeak by for another month and access food stamps to buy the bare necessities. Even with my family members working until their fingers bled, there just wasn't enough provision to make ends meet.

A lot of people think that poverty is the result of poor planning, but poverty teaches you that planning is futile. I remember one time I saved up seventeen dollars in pennies for car insurance, but then the electricity got shut off and my meager months of saving had to go to the most immediate need. Why even plan ahead in the first place?

The best analogy I can give is that living in poverty feels like being in a war. You're constantly fighting against a phantom that steals your hope and any joy you could feel for life and makes you live in constant fear. Poverty pits people against each other, because every group thinks that the "others" are getting all of the best jobs, the help, tutoring in school and the government aid. The whites think the blacks, Latinos, and Native Americans are getting the help and vice versa. When I would enroll in a new school in a new town, I'd get beaten up on the playground because the other kids thought that I was just a "rich white girl."

Poverty was a cruel teacher, and had driven home the lesson that this kind of life was all there was.

Martin Luther King Jr. talked a lot about this underlying hate, understanding that economic injustices could compound the divide in this country. I tell people now, "If you've ever been hungry, I'm your sister. If you've been evicted, we're related." I have more in common with those people, regardless of race, than with those who grew up with a consistent roof over their head or with food in the fridge.

I was an okay student. I liked writing, and some of my teachers even told me I had a true talent with words, but school didn't pay any of the bills or put a crumb of food on the table. So I dropped out after my freshman year (after all, the family had just gotten evicted), and I figured I could work to help do my part. Anyway, my mom only had an eighth grade education and what did I need school for anyway, if my only aspiration was to survive and maybe be a wife and a mother? Poverty was a cruel teacher, and had driven home the lesson that this kind of life was all there was.

I reached my goal pretty quickly. I married another migrant worker when I was just fifteen, giving my mom and stepfather one less mouth to feed. We had our honeymoon in a cherry field and started the cycle again: working that day for food for that night. But it wasn't the life of unconditional love I'd hoped to find. By twenty-one, I'd had two miscarriages, a four-year-old daughter (Jennifer), a two-year-old son (Daniel), and a marriage it was pretty clear wasn't going to survive the plague of dead-end jobs and sky-high piles of bills.

By the time I was twenty-six, I was divorced, my ex-husband offering no support for our two little children or me. I had a ninth-grade education and no job skills. I received $408 in welfare and food stamps each month. By the time I paid $395 in rent for a tiny, decrepit apartment, I had $13 left to pay for everything else. You know how that ends, right? When I told my social worker about the eviction notice on my front door, she yelled at me, demanding I take a government-funded money-management course. I thought, *I'm sure I could manage it better, if there were just MORE of it!*

I heard the familiar voice in my head, telling me I was stupid, lazy, and a failure at everything I'd tried to do. I went to the county relief agency, where a man in wiry glasses told me—from the other side of a Plexiglas shield, as if my "disease" of poverty might rub off on him—that all he could do for me was pay my electric bill for one month. Can you imagine? They were offering to pay a bill at an apartment I was about to be kicked out of. I slumped down in my chair, another familiar wave of defeat washing over me. *Look at me*, I thought. *I'm forty pounds overweight, a single mom, and I'm about to be homeless again.*

A woman stepped forward and tapped me on the shoulder. I jumped. Judy Gibland introduced herself, looking at my face, even though my eyes were pointed straight down at the floor. She told me she thought she could help, and shared some basic details about a three-week intensive life skills training course for homemakers, or in my case, single mothers. I basically told her to shove it. She didn't take it personally, knowing my reaction had nothing to do with her but was learned behavior from a lifetime of poverty. She insisted that I take the number and pressed a card into my hand, in case it might be helpful in the future.

I stormed out, thinking, *Who does this woman think she is? She doesn't know anything about my situation or me. She looked all put together and obviously has*

no experience with being poor. Poverty taught me
attitude, like putting on armor to insulate me from
the judgment of those who didn't understand. On
my way back to the apartment, I saw a fast-food
restaurant. I thought, *That's probably the best I can
hope for, working in a pizza place.* I pulled the card
out of my purse and found a pay phone. I figured,
at least I could get the voucher for a few months of
free subsidized housing if I completed the course.
What did I have to lose?

I started the Women in Transition program with
a huge chip on my shoulder. I didn't know when to
say "seen" or "saw," "went" or "gone," and every other
word was "ain't." Even though the others in my class
looked like me, dressed in thrift store clothes with
bad dye jobs or perms, I still thought, *No one here
knows me.* That all changed when Suzannah Mercer,
one of the program's organizers, strode to the
podium one day.

She was flawless. Her pale blonde hair was tucked
back in a tasteful chignon. She wore a soft, knee-
length floral dress with a single pearl around her
elegant, swanlike neck. She began to tell her own
personal story, one that sounded familiar to me.
She was born into poverty, and had been a single
mom, divorced and on welfare. But she escaped and
had completed a college degree, and was now helping others make the same escape. I couldn't believe
that this stunning creature could have had a past like
mine. For the first time I thought, *Maybe I can do*

the same. Maybe there is something else out there for me. I dared to hope.

"If you could have any job in the world, what would it be?" No one had ever asked me any such thing before.

The Women in Transition program took a comprehensive, connected approach, meeting people where they were, rather than where the organizers wanted them to be. I was treated with respect and dignity by people who understood that the way I spoke wasn't an indication of a low IQ. We learned financial skills, yes, but there was a high concentration on rebuilding self-esteem, something poverty had stripped from me. We learned of various programs available to allow us to get our high school equivalency certificate and maybe, if we wanted and were willing to work hard, a college degree.

One of the things that was most different about the group of four amazing women running the program was that they encouraged us to really dream and told us that no dream was too big. They asked, "If you could have any job in the world, what would it be?" No one had ever asked me any such thing before. I blurted out, "I'd like to be just like Mary Hart on *Entertainment Tonight* on TV!"

Rather than laughing in my face and pointing out that I could barely put together a sentence that wasn't riddled with grammatical mistakes, Judy said, "That's great, Donna. It sounds like you might be interested in studying journalism." There it was again—an unfamiliar glimmer of hope.

I took that shred of hope and the voucher for free temporary housing and scraped together enough money and willpower to get my GED. With the help of my mentors, I navigated the process of applying for student aid and to Mount Hood Community College. I was so excited to share the news with my state-appointed welfare caseworker, but instead of being thrilled for me as I'd expected, her face fell flat. "You can't do that," she said. "If you enroll in college, we'll have to cut your monthly welfare check *way* back." Can you imagine? I was already barely scraping by and trying to find a way out of the cycle of government assistance with college. I felt like they were trying to keep me trapped. "Cut me, then," I responded. I'd just have to find a way to make it work and go to school.

My check went from $408 each month down to $250 for my little family of three. I started going to classes and got evicted yet again. My mentors helped me find another voucher to live in a ramshackle motel surrounded by drug dealers and crime, and my mom kept my children as often as she could. It felt like I was walking the thinnest tightrope you could imagine, trying desperately to get across a divide to a better life.

I enrolled in journalism classes and published an article in the school paper. My grammar was still a constant struggle, but when someone would use a word I didn't know, I'd pretend I did, secretly writing it down. Then I'd go to the library, look up words like "acrimonious," "propagate," and "nascent," memorizing their meanings and how to use them in a sentence. I studied hard at night and juggled food stamps to feed Jennifer, Daniel, and myself. When I walked across the stage at graduation, I became the first person in my family to earn an associate's degree. I felt another unfamiliar emotion: pride.

Even as it felt like the world was opening up to me, I heard the ever-present doubts rise up. I'd been able to find Section 8 housing, but I could barely keep up with the monthly payments. I'd already cut down to the barest of basics, doing without even a telephone for emergencies. Should I quit now and try to find another husband and a passable job? *No way*, I thought. I enrolled in the bachelor's program at the University of Portland in the fall of 1988.

If I'd been among my peers at the tiny community college, I felt like a fish out of water at the sprawling University of Portland campus. I walked to class among freshly scrubbed students, sporting their latest fashions and stylish book bags. I was older than they and still wearing thrift store finds. My professors knew immediately that I was a hard worker, but I always felt so demoralized when I got papers back with comments like, "Great points in here, Donna, but your grammar is atrocious."

Dr. Bob Fulford, one of my professors, pulled me aside one day after class and said, "I see how hard you're working and how intelligent you are, but I've noticed that sometimes you have some challenges with your grammar. Would you like me to help you?" It was the lifeline I needed. I accepted and started meeting with him regularly, submitting to his gentle correction and permanently erasing "ain't" from my vocabulary. I found a job on campus that allowed me time to study and slowly weaned myself off welfare.

In 1989, Dr. Fulford learned that my brother Wayne was in prison and asked if he could visit him. On that visit, the superintendent shared that his organization was struggling with the effects of poverty on people in prison. Dr. Fulford told him that he and I could develop trainings that would improve communication and relationships across poverty and race barriers. He asked me if I'd want to start a consulting business with him and I said "Absolutely!" joking that I'd like to be the president of our little venture. Always encouraging my aspirations, he had two sets of business cards made, naming me president and him VP. Communication Across Barriers was born, and the State of Oregon Department of Corrections became our first client.

> Together, we developed a ten-week curriculum that included videos, workbooks, and facilitator guides to help improve relationships and communication across poverty barriers.
>
> I graduated with honors, went on to earn a master's degree in communication with a minor in gender studies (with honors), and a doctorate degree in educational leadership.

In her class that day, Donna told her story while the students sat with their mouths hanging open, trying to wrap their minds around the incongruous idea of their polished professor wading through the mire of poverty, homelessness, and hunger. She said, "We're the only country in the world that teaches that *you're* the cause of your own poverty. Other countries are honest about access to jobs, excellent childcare, teaching, and learning."

Donna continues, "Here in the United States, though, you find an internalizing of the poverty, so that the poor, especially those in generational poverty, where everyone they know or have access to is just like them, are not only poor but also ashamed. In most other countries around the world, poor people still have their pride, dignity, and confidence. Americans and the media have created this notion that people are poor because they've made bad choices. Often, they are so mired in a cycle that seems unbreakable and the non-poverty-stricken people around them may as well be a part of another country entirely."

Donna's accomplishments in this area are incredible! January 2015 marked her twenty-fifth year as president of Communication Across Barriers. She has worked in all fifty states and written two books: *See Poverty . . . Be the Difference* and *Breaking Poverty Barriers to Equal Justice*. Donna has been named a Princeton Fellow, and Portland State University has named their new School of Social Work building in her honor.

All of Donna's effort is dedicated to ensuring people have authentic opportunities to move out and stay out of the poverty war zone. She's helped countless numbers of people she doesn't know, but some of her most striking contributions have been within her own family. Two of her brothers hold bachelor's degrees, several of her cousins—some of whose parents can still only sign an X for their names—are entering graduate school, and her son is a proud business owner. Her example has created positive ripples that will improve generations to come.

Donna sums it up perfectly at the conclusion of her seminar, saying, "*We* have to be the ones to create understanding of the *people* who suffer in this poverty cycle and offer them a path out, just as the Women in Transition program and openhearted people like Dr. Fulford did for me."

Will you be one to make a difference?

REACT

How would you answer the questions "What do you think of the homeless?" and "What do you think about a homeless person?"

TAKE ACTION

WHAT CAN **ONE** DO?
Make a connection

I HOPE THAT BY READING STORIES about those who have overcome poverty you are inspired to see the potential and dignity of each person despite their difficult circumstances. Reading these stories just isn't enough. To really understand and make a difference in the midst of the complexities of poverty, it is vital to make time to get to know someone in poverty. To make this personal, try following these steps:

Investigate what is happening in your local community in the area of poverty. Connect with an organization doing good work with people who are struggling with poverty.

Ask the organization if you could become a friend to one person or one family.

Create opportunities to get acquainted just as if you were meeting a new friend.

Share your life story as appropriate.

Be conversational, seeking common ground. Don't just focus on issues of poverty.

Discover their language of affirmation. In other words, what motivates this person or family? For example, if a child is consistently late for school (due to a variety of factors you may or may not know about), instead of saying, "You're late again," try "We're so glad you're here. You're going to learn so much today!"

As you walk alongside this person and share conversations, meals, experiences, and sometimes frustrations, you will create solutions for *one*.

WHAT CAN MORE THAN **ONE** DO?
Homeless for a night

James Barnett worked at J.P. Morgan Chase Bank with a lucrative income until January 1, 2010. That day, James began an unlikely adventure. He intentionally chose to be homeless. James told me that he wanted to understand all that is a part of homelessness and poverty. He spent the next two years in many cities across the United States living in poverty and homelessness.

James recounted that the first night he took to the streets in Atlanta, he realized what he and many people had romanticized about was not what he expected. The first thing James had to do was hide what gear he owned so that it wouldn't be stolen. James ate his dinner at a local soup kitchen. Doug, one of the first guys James met, made it clear to James that he must secure at least two or three layers of cardboard to stay warm overnight. It was evident this would be a reality that would change his preconceptions about the condition of homelessness. Here are portions of his story:

James's Story:

I met Doug soon after I arrived under the bridge. He told me that the best way to secure my "shelter" was to go dumpster diving near a college campus, so off we went. Once we had our cardboard and retrieved our property, we found a spot under a streetlight, near a building, and far away from the road so we wouldn't be picked up by the police.

I'll never forget that first night. I certainly didn't sleep well. I woke up at one point and thought about my need for a bathroom break, but realized that would be impossible, since there were so many people packed in around me.

The people I met that night, and many after, really surprised me. Some were homeless out of generational poverty, but so many were in this situation due to factors like the downturn of the economy, divorce, medical bills, and even as the result of a fire, where the family lost everything. What I also experienced was unbelievable compassion and care across the community.

A story that brought this caring culture front and center was during a time while James was in Gainesville, Florida. James met Tony and Judy, who took him to their tent city. This "city" actually had a guest tent where James stayed for the evening!

James has numerous stories and lessons learned from his journey. James doesn't recommend that everyone take his path, but encourages you to find a safe way to spend the night with those who are homeless and experience a transformation of your thinking and heart for people in poverty.

Here are our suggestions:

Secure a location and nonprofit to work alongside.

Inspire your circle of influence to spend one evening as a homeless person with you.

Ask people to sponsor your homeless evening.

Get to know one person during the evening in a respectful way.

Journal your experience and feelings and share with those who sponsored you.

Donate funds raised to an organization working with those in poverty.

Consider continuing to connect with a person you met on your night of homelessness.

Poverty simulation

Invite your circle of influence to a Poverty Simulation Event.

Ask guests to wear something that is old and dirty.

Most people living in poverty do not have a full-service grocery store near them and rely on convenience stores for their staples. Serve "convenient type" foods (potato chips, taquitos, candy, sodas, etc.).

Engage in a Poverty Simulation using one of these resources:

Contact Action Ministries to schedule a Poverty Simulation: http://actionministries.net

Explore Market Place and use their interactive simulation to lead the group: http://www.marketplace.org/topics /wealth-poverty/could-you-live-438-week

Secure kits from Missouri Community Action Network: http:// www.communityaction.org/Poverty%20Simulation.aspx

Enlist a group to run the event for you by connecting with Hope Link: https://www.hope-link.org/take_action /poverty_simulation/

At the end of the simulation, share experiences.

As a group, choose an action that could impact families in poverty.

TEACH **ONE**
Where did the money go?

I asked my friend Jenn Henn to share a learning experience she had with her son. You'll learn a lot from Jenn and her son Jacob.

Jenn's Story:

Our family lives in the suburbs of Atlanta and rarely comes in contact with anyone who is experiencing poverty. About five years ago, I began volunteering with the girls at Wellspring Living. I was horrified at the idea that little girls could be bought and sold in my city, and I felt like I needed to do something. So my friends and I, determined to make a difference, packed up our scrapbooking supplies and traveled south forty-five minutes to the Wellspring Living home.

What I discovered on those Saturdays was that horrible things had happened to these precious girls, and their life circumstances, most living well below the poverty line, set them up to be vulnerable to trafficking.

I'm a typical mom making sure my children are in good schools, eating well, dressed appropriately, and involved in sports and other extracurricular activities they enjoy. I could not reconcile with myself the disparity of how my children were growing up and what was happening with the girls I scrapbooked with on Saturdays. Even more, I became concerned that my children had no idea what was going on around them, so I began to look for opportunities to broaden their horizons about the "real world" to encourage empathy, compassion, and maybe, they too would want to tangibly do something to make a difference. Mary Frances shared an interactive online experience on the website: http://playspent.org as an avenue to help teenagers see what it is like to live in poverty on a thousand dollars for a month.

I asked my sixteen-year-old son, Jacob, to take the PLAYSPENT Challenge, and what an eye-opening experience it was. At each screen, Jacob has to make decisions. At each decision, a tally is kept of how much of his thousand dollars was left, and then another life choice was waiting at the next screen. On the first screen, Jacob chose to work as a waiter. The next screen revealed that even with tips he only made eight dollars an hour. Jacob was completely surprised! Then he had the rude awakening of how much money in taxes was taken out. He was realizing he had to be very careful with how he spent every penny, so Jacob chose the cheapest health insurance, hoping that his family wouldn't get sick and eventually decided that he just wouldn't ever go to the doctor.

Going grocery shopping on Day 9 was just awful. "Wait, the cheaper food is unhealthy!"

When Jacob got to Day 4 he said, "Wait, how am I going to make it through the whole month with just this much money?" Each day was a new challenging situation.

Day 7, Jacob became very upset about getting a write-up for missing work because he went to apply for a scholarship for his child. Going grocery shopping on Day 9 was just awful. "Wait, the cheaper food is unhealthy!"

On Day 12, his little girl was supposed to go to a birthday party. "I feel really bad about sending my kid to a birthday party without a gift, but I can't afford a gift and don't want my child to miss the party." Since money was running out, Jacob turned to get food stamps. The news was not good. "What, I can't get food stamps until next month? How will I buy food?"

On Day 15, Jacob realized, "I don't get any more paychecks this month." Later that month, Jacob was in a traffic accident. "I had to drive away after I hit another car, because there was no way I could pay for the damage," he explained. Jacob realized other complexities during his trek through thirty days of living in poverty:

It's not fair for my kid.

I couldn't go to see his play at school because of the extra job I had to take.

I can't pay my college loan and now have to pay 15 percent interest!

I owe $7300 in credit card debt and I can't pay anything.

As Jacob finished up his thirty days, he told me, "It just seems like a vicious cycle. I miss work to help my child and I could get fired. I can't afford to take an extra online class to help get myself out of this. It's exasperating and frustrating."

I think his empathy has been built. Now we are going to explore ways Jacob can get involved in breaking this vicious cycle.

Jenn and Jacob encourage you to build understanding with your children by completing this interactive experience on-line: http://playspent.org (Once you get on the site, click the arrow: CONTINUE TO SPENT). We hope you have valuable conversations to build empathy and engagement in the issue of poverty.

Building relationships

Connect with a local organization that reaches out to those in poverty. Follow these steps to build an intentional relationship.

Build a relationship with a family closely matching yours.

Make intentional visits at least once a month.

Sponsor an activity away from their shelter/home to have family fun together. (Enjoy a picnic at a park, take a trip to the zoo or historical site, or just enjoy a meal together.)

Commit to monthly activities for one year.

Take time after each visit to journal and discuss with your children the experience, focusing on finding common ground, dignity, and hope.

What if the two families will become connected in a "forever" relationship?

15.8 million children in the United States lived in food-insecure households in 2013.[1]

In 2013, 44 percent of all Supplemental Nutrition Assistance Program (SNAP) participants were children under the age of eighteen.[2]

Three out of four teachers say their students regularly come to school hungry.[3]

PART TWO

ZERO HUNGER

---

1. the uneasy or painful sensation caused by want of food; craving appetite. Also the exhausted condition caused by want of food

2. the want or scarcity of food in a country

3. a strong desire or craving

CHAPTER 5

ONE HUNGER GAME, WON

If you can't feed a hundred people,
then feed just one.
—MOTHER TERESA

RUTH RILEY is the kind of woman who stands out in almost any crowd and not for the obvious reasons. She cuts a striking figure, towering over both men and women at 6 foot, 4 ½ inches, so it's unbelievable to think that she's ever been at risk for being hungry or lacking proper nutrition.

She was a star center basketball player for Notre Dame, helping the college win the national title in 2001. She helped Team USA bring home gold in the 2004 Summer Olympics in Athens, Greece, and has played for WNBA teams including the Atlanta Dream, Miami Sol, Chicago Sky, San Antonio Silver Stars, and the Detroit Shock, where she helped win not one, but two WNBA World Championship titles.

More than any of that, though, she's someone who lives her life with passion, determination, conviction, and purpose.

When you see Ruth's impressive list of accomplishments, it might be easy to assume that she lived a charmed childhood, one filled with pricey basketball camps, personal trainers, and easy access to anything her young heart desired. Instead, the reality was that growing up, Ruth had a very close brush with hunger—to which one in five children in America can relate—and it has inspired her to make an impact for children who struggle with food insecurity every day. Here's her story.

Ruth's Story:

I was born in 1979 in Ransom, Kansas. I have an older sister, Rachel, and a younger brother, Jake. My dad left when I was four years old, offering little to no support, so my mom, Sharon, moved our family to Macy, Indiana, where she grew up. She was a superhard worker, but she wasn't really trained to do a highly skilled, and thus, better paying, job. In her family, the boys were encouraged to get an education, but the girls were not. So all that was available to her were low-paying jobs. For a time, she operated a little beauty shop out of our house. Other times, she worked in factories or as a dishwasher at the local diner, sometimes taking on two or even three jobs to make sure that we were taken care of and had what we needed.

No matter what she did, though, there was only ever enough money to barely squeak by. I can just imagine how many silent tears she cried. As a child, I was pretty clueless to the level of poverty we were

living in, since my mom mercifully shielded my
siblings and me from the realities of bill paying and
financial stress. I'll always be grateful to her for that,
and I'm in awe of the kind of burden she took on
herself, so we could enjoy our childhoods. It was a
gift, one that I realize many lower-income children
don't enjoy.

Though we lived at or below the poverty line, I always felt loved and cared for, my mom miraculously
finding a way to keep food on the table. Looking
back on my childhood, probably one of the food-
related ways I felt poverty the most was in the lack
of variety in our diets. Instead of lots of different
kinds of foods that my classmates brought in their
lunches, I tended to have the standard peanut butter and jelly sandwich and maybe a piece of fruit. I
remember one time, in second grade, a friend's mom
packed her a kiwi as a snack and I had no idea what
it was. I'd never seen that bright green fruit with
fuzzy skin and tiny jet-black seeds. It was delicious.

People at school described me with obvious words
like "tall," "lanky," and "uncoordinated." After all,
I was six feet tall by the time I was twelve. Those
who knew me a little better also said I was "shy" and
"self-conscious." The one that always stung a bit was
"poor," even though I knew it was true. I watched
as my mom counted every penny and did without
things I know she would have loved to get.

As I got older, I started to realize how different
my family was from everyone else. We were off

and on food stamps, WIC (special supplemental nutrition program for Women, Infants, and Children), *free* and reduced lunches, and sometimes breakfasts at school. Sadly, there is sometimes a negative stigma around those programs that can keep children from feeling comfortable to participate and receive the necessary provision. My mom reassured my siblings and me that we were smart, talented, and on a path to do great things.

When young people aren't well fed it can compromise their ability to learn, their focus is diminished and of course, their ability to perform in athletics is cut way down.

By the time I was a freshman in high school, I was a lot taller than all of the girls (and many of the boys, for that matter!), which only added to my self-consciousness. I was teased for my towering height, so I internalized a lot of things, withdrawing into a shell. However, my self-esteem began to grow exponentially with my budding interest in and aptitude for basketball. My sister ran cross-country and my brother played basketball and football, so we were a pretty athletic bunch.

My mother modeled the example of hard work, and I applied those lessons on the court. Good nutrition became even more important for me as I also worked hard to excel in academics. I know that when young people aren't well fed it can compromise their ability to learn, their focus is diminished and of course, their ability to perform in athletics is cut way down. Playing basketball, along with studying hard, was my ticket, and I received a scholarship to attend my dream college, Notre Dame. After graduation, I was drafted to the Miami Sol WNBA team and my career took me to places like Europe, Asia, and Africa. I could have never imagined this as a poor farm girl in north Indiana.

In 2012, at the NBA All-Star Jam Session, I was introduced to Share Our Strength[4] for the first time. It's a national nonprofit committed to ending childhood hunger in America by making sure kids in need have access to nutritious food. It invests in community organizations fighting hunger, teaches families how to make dollars stretch to buy and prepare healthy meals within their budgets and builds partnerships between the public and private sectors to end hunger on a state and national level.

When I stopped by their booth to take the No Kid Hungry pledge, it struck me how grateful I was that I'd been able to access the programs I needed to get the nutrition necessary to achieve my goals. I found out that the No Kid Hungry program was launching their Illinois initiative later that year and, after hearing my personal near-hunger story, they asked me to be a part of it. I spoke at the official launch, and with the backing of the NBA and WNBA, the charity helped connect more than fifty thousand youth across the United States to urgently needed free meals that summer. Share Our Strength recognizes that for many children, summer is the hungriest time of the year.

One thing I've noticed, again and again as I've been involved in raising awareness on the issue of hunger, is that it's not a glamorous one and you can't readily see when a child is hungry or isn't getting all of the nutrition he or she needs. After all, when most people hear "hunger" they think of starving children in the developing world. However, it's a reality facing nearly 16 million kids in the United States. Without the necessary food, kids lose the ability to dream and to set goals for a better future— these are things we shouldn't expect them to live without, especially not in America.

We all have our own unique area of influence.

I've heard over and over again that there isn't a shortage of food in this country or a shortage of programs to feed those in need, but rather, there's a shortage of access. There needs to be a greater focus to increase participation in existing programs and to remove the stigma children feel in participating. We want this country's children to be strong, smart, and successful, so we need to be instrumental in helping them get there. I'll be forever grateful for having a strong mother who knew how to get us the nutritional help we needed growing up. It's truly changed my life.

The beautiful thing about acts of kindness is that you don't have to be a professional athlete to have a platform or to do something good. We all have our own unique area of influence, and mine has been shaped by my faith and my upbringing and then extended out by the sport that I play. I hope that by telling my story of food insecurity growing up that families, and especially children, will know that some of their favorite professional players have struggled in some of the very same ways they are. I hope that by shining a light on this issue, I'm encouraging kids to dream dreams well beyond their current circumstances. History doesn't have to continually repeat itself—sometimes it just needs to be rewritten.

Ruth's story is so powerful because it's easy to imagine it going another way, especially if she hadn't had a strong mother who was willing to do whatever it took for her children to get the sustenance they needed to excel. So many children aren't as fortunate.

I've heard it more times than I can count. A young woman who has been living in the worst kind of slavery—right here in this country—tells her story and it includes "I trusted him because I was hungry, and he was the only one who offered me anything to eat." Or, "I hadn't had any food for a couple of days and this seemingly nice guy bought me a Happy Meal." It's heartbreaking that the gnawing pit in one's stomach could be the thing that snares her in the clutches of a trafficker.

Food is the most basic of needs, second only to water to drink, and it's a tragedy that in one of the greatest countries in the world, the United States, so many of our people, children included, are hungry or food insecure. You might think that the issue of hunger is unrelated to the issue of risk or trafficking, but I can assure you, the two are woven together. Will you be one who makes a difference?

REACT

How can simple hunger affect a child or teen? (Think of school performance, fear, even being fooled into trusting a stranger for a meal.) Were you surprised at the number of hungry children in the United States?

CHAPTER 6

ONE GOOD MEAL NOURISHES THE SOUL

Hunger is truly mankind's war of liberation.
—JOHN FITZGERALD KENNEDY

CAN YOU REMEMBER the last time you were truly hungry? I'm not talking about the twinge of discomfort that happens when there's a long wait at your favorite restaurant. I'm talking about the gnawing pit in your stomach that grows after days of undernourishment. I hope you *can't* remember that feeling. Unfortunately, though, it's a reality for millions right here in America—one of the most developed nations in the world. Hunger's a powerful motivator, but it's also an ailment you can't see. In fact, some of the victims you'll read about on these very pages found themselves under the control of a trafficker after simply accepting a meal.

Perhaps the silver lining of this great need is that it motivates people to make an impact in a big way. Dave Phillips is just such a man. This issue of hunger as the most basic of needs has captured his heart. More than that, though, he's come to see providing food as a way to build relationships, positive relationships that can help bridge the gap between poverty and provision, unemployment and a secure job, isolation and community. He knows it's possible because he's seen it work hundreds—maybe thousands—of times through his Los Angeles–based organization, Children's Hunger Fund. Here is his story.

Dave's Story:

I didn't grow up with hunger or food insecurity in my Southern California home, but because my parents prioritized serving others, I was exposed to very real needs in my own backyard early on. When I was eleven years old, I began working with my dad to serve the needs of the poor in South Central Los Angeles.

Geographically, my area was a study in opposites: within a couple of miles were some of the most affluent neighborhoods in the whole country, but also some of the poorest and most desperate. Plus, it was like a microcosm of the world, with so many cultures colliding. It seemed that as many people didn't speak English as did. Throughout my teenage years, I heard stories of how people came to be homeless or hungry and, as I built relationships, my heart was bent toward service and making a difference.

Like most of my high school peers, though, I left for college to study something "productive." I chose international banking and when I graduated, I found a job in a fast-paced start-up company, managing the creation and distribution of educational toys. My role offered terrific exposure to the business world, but I felt like there was something more for me. This idea was further cemented in my mind as a result of a short-term trip I took to Honduras and Guatemala.

As I traveled to Central America, I worked with orphans and spent time at a Love and Life Center for children with cancer. It was the first time I'd been exposed to poverty and suffering in that way. Near the end of my trip, I visited a children's home for terminal cancer patients, run by one caring couple. There were sixty children, for whom there was no hope of a cure short of a miracle. My heart broke wide open as I struggled to wrap my twenty-four-year-old mind around these tragic, impossible circumstances.

While I wanted to make a difference for any child who had a need, I realized how great the need was in my own hometown.

While I wanted to make a difference for any child who had a need, I realized how great the need was in my own hometown. While working for World Opportunities, a nonprofit in Hollywood,

California, I was tasked with starting an inner-city feeding program, targeting low-income housing projects in Watts, like Jordan Downs, Nickerson, and Imperial Courts. I sought out wholesale food companies, produce brokers, and bakeries for fresh bread, fresh produce, and staples like rice, canned food, and so forth. The whole operation got huge in a hurry. Within three years we were distributing about three hundred tons of food each week to 150 agencies around the city and throughout Southern California.

During this time, I became aware of the complexities of poverty and hunger in inner cities, and I began to see what a powerful tool food can be in order to build relationships. Still, I felt a bit like a hamster on a wheel, running around giving out food, without really changing anything about the factors that kept people in a cycle of poverty and hunger in the first place. I wanted—needed—to do more.

Rather than thinking of the poor as a number, we wanted to think of them as individuals with unique hopes, dreams, and skills.

I was married to my wonderful wife, Lynn, by this time. She was a schoolteacher and she too wanted to see our community change, one hungry person at a time. So in December 1991, we stepped out on faith and agreed to live on her salary for a time, and to delay our goals of starting a family and buying a house. I quit my job to start Children's Hunger Fund. It was born out of a bedroom office and our garage.

From the beginning, the vision was simple. I would reach out to corporations who were in a position to contribute either food or funds to buy food. Then we would partner with churches to distribute the provisions to people in need. We wanted to try and help the church experience a paradigm shift. Up until that time (really beginning during the Great Depression in this country), most feeding programs involved a family or individual coming to a location, standing in line, and taking away food. It always seemed to be some version of this, whether it be in a hot meal program, a brown bag program, or food pantry, However, all of these things were extremely low-contact and weren't highly relational. Beyond that, though, they tended to create dependency and chipped away at the dignity of the families served, particularly when those people were treated as clients or just a number.

It seemed so obvious, but relationships could be the lynchpin, the missing element for organizations to help motivate sustained positive life change. Rather than thinking of the poor as a number, we wanted to think of them as individuals with unique hopes, dreams, and skills. Ultimately, we believed that this was the way the church—and human decency and kindness—was designed to work in the first place.

We built a home delivery model of engagement, providing training to churches to pass along to their members. Basically, it should work like this: someone notices a family or an individual in the community who needs help. They could be homeless, out of work, or simply underemployed. They help address the most immediate need by delivering a Food Pak every week or two, filled with basics like rice, canned food, fresh fruit and vegetables, cereal, pasta, and more. As trust and understanding are built, typically other factors in poverty come to light. Often opportunities arise to help in tangible ways, such as filling out job applications, gaining literacy training, job skills training, and help connecting to legal aid. It's a holistic approach, one that works because both parties involved are personally vested.

One of my favorite success stories of how this works is about a young woman named Kim Bowser. Kim was a recent graduate of the University of California and noticed a family of five in her Hollywood neighborhood that was sleeping in their car. The family—a mom, dad, and three young children—accepted her offer to deliver Food Paks from time to time.

As she got to know the Hernandez family, even through their broken English and her broken Spanish, she came to love them. She learned of Mr. Hernandez's struggle to find sustainable employment and helped him find a better job. The economic lift alone for this one family has been exponential.

Through additional resources at her church, Kim was able to help the Hernandez family connect with opportunities for housing. When they moved into an apartment, she held a fundraiser to help furnish it, giving the two boys their own beds with mattresses for the first time since they moved to the States. She's taken the children to sporting events, day trips out of the city, and to school functions. Their lives are woven together now, so much so that two of the children, Roberto and Abby, were the ring bearer and flower girl in her wedding. Now Food Paks are rarely a part of their interaction, but they were the catalyst to a lifelong friendship.

Hunger is trauma, and when food has been scarce, the aftereffects can last a lifetime.

For a while, our California facility was across from a subsidized housing project. I was leaving work one night and saw a little boy of eight clutching a baggie and yelling up to his friends, who were hanging out of third-floor windows. I couldn't hear what he was saying, but I could tell that he was yelling something—a question, maybe—and they were shaking their heads no. I pulled over and introduced myself and asked him what he was doing and what he needed. He showed me the contents of his tattered plastic bag: three lonely, crumbling crackers, which Moises explained a friend had given him at school that day. He knew that was all he would have to eat that evening or the next morning, since his mom would be working her second job late into the night, so he was checking to see if any of his friends had a spoonful of peanut butter to make his "meal" stretch further. He told me, through his tears, that on any given day, he doesn't know where his next meal will come from. Talk about emotional trauma. That night, I made sure he and his single mom were connected with a local church, which had the resources to help care for this little family of two, until they were able to provide consistently for themselves.

As you can see from Moises's story, hunger is trauma, and when food has been scarce, the aftereffects can last a lifetime. It creates a survivor mentality, one that can manifest in food hoarding and distrust. Hungry children often exhibit emotional, developmental, and educational delays. They are disadvantaged in the classroom, which hurts their development during the critical years in school. In fact, hungry children are often labeled with a learning disorder when the heart of the issue could be undernourishment. Education is the single greatest path out of generational poverty and yet it's nearly impossible for children to latch on and make the most of it when they can't focus on anything else but the loud growl of hunger in their bellies.

It's tempting to think that hunger isn't a real factor in America, the land of the free. This is just not true.

Ultimately, with Children's Hunger Fund, we wanted to create a movement in this country and beyond, a bridge that could cultivate understanding through acts of mercy. We want to help create an environment where every child in America has the ability to hope and dream of a better future. In 2014, we helped distribute 19 million meals in the United States, from our three distribution centers (Los Angeles, Texas, and Illinois). We are planning to add another one in the South in 2015 and we're hoping more after that.

Whether or not you're a churchgoing person or if there's a Children's Hunger Fund distribution center in your region, I encourage everyone to build a relationship, a bridge, to get to know someone who is outside of your comfort zone. Share a meal if you're able, but share your skills and your knowledge and share hope. You never know if that interaction will be what nourishes a hungry soul.

TAKE ACTION

WHAT CAN **ONE** DO?
Become involved and informed

DID YOU KNOW Americans spend $61 billion on pet food as compared to the $50 billion our country spends to feed hungry people? To become involved with reducing hunger, it is important that you learn all you can. Here are some steps:

Check out the Gift Catalog for Children's Hunger Fund: http://catalog.childrenshungerfund.org

Become informed about hunger. Toolkits are available on Feeding America's website: http://www.feedingamerica.org/

Volunteer at your local food bank.

No Kid Hungry Campaign outlines eleven things you can do at this website: http://actioncenter.nokidhungry.org/actions/partner/no-kid-hungry

WHAT CAN MORE THAN **ONE** DO?
Lunch bunch

In 2011, Emily Brewer had just become a mom for the first time and wasn't planning to return to teaching. Emily loved children and wanted to do something to make a difference, so when she found out about a need at her church for a lunch bunch director, she applied.

Not really knowing all that was involved, Emily began working to create lunches in the summer for children in her county who were on free and reduced lunches during the school term. Years earlier, the program began when the county leadership at the Department of Children and Family Services reached out to churches, synagogues, and mosques to ask for their assistance in providing lunches. A group was asked to provide lunches one day a week and deliver them to the homes of the children where parents had given permission.

The first summer, Emily led a group of committed volunteers to prepare and deliver 120 lunches. Last summer, seven hundred lunches were prepared and delivered weekly to each home by volunteers. When I asked Emily how she got so many volunteers and so many donations, she commented, "Our church provides a budget for perishables, but the other items are donated. When I have a need, I blast it on social media, and we seem to have enough every week." Emily told me that many children would tell their teachers at the end of the school year they hated summer because they knew they would be hungry. Because of the industrious work of a mom (now with two boys), children are not insecure about their meals over the summer.

Share a meal

My friend Michael Campbell introduced me to Amanda Hindson, who often joined his team to take dinner to a men's program in Atlanta. She put her experiences into such a moving piece that I wanted to let you read her words. You will be inspired!

Amanda's Story:

Yesterday I made four pounds of black-eyed peas. That's a lot of peas to contend with. The two largest pots I own were filled nearly to the brim. Jon and I along with some of our friends were headed to Trinity House, a place where men—called Brothers—can restart their lives. Dinner is brought to Trinity House nightly by different groups of volunteers. We had been recruited, and our assignment was to bring black-eyed peas.

Upon arrival at the house, we are instantly greeted by a smiling face—my one-hundred-pound pots of peas whisked away into the kitchen. The lobby is elegant and cozy, with a painting of Dr. King proudly displayed on the walls. We pass the glowing, stained-glass windows of the chapel and land in the middle of the hustle and bustle with lots of chatter and laughter as dinner is being assembled and strangers introduced.

The evening begins with a tour of the facility. Our tour guide, Saeed, takes us around and explains the program, the men, the history as well as the meaning and symbolism that is deeply rooted and woven into the program. After the tour, we all sit down for dinner, volunteers and Brothers evenly dispersed around the chapel. Everyone dines on some delicious soul food: green beans, black-eyed peas, rolls, salad, and fried chicken. As dinner wraps up, the time for stories begins. Everyone has a turn, including the volunteers. I was moved as I listened to the stories of the Brothers in the house; some with master's degrees, former business professionals, fathers, husbands, chefs, project managers, musicians—men from all paths and places. You cannot judge appearance; you never know a person's story unless you *hear* it— every created human being has dignity.

The atmosphere in the room is not sad or heavy. It is filled with laughter and noise and hope and joy and acceptance and love. We hear stories of dark pasts, future plans, hopes, and dreams. We laugh and clap and dance and sing. We are humbled. We are inspired.

And all I offered was black-eyed peas for twenty-five. I left feeling whole, joyful, hopeful, glowing with all of the knowledge and inspiration that the men of Trinity House had offered to me.

TEACH **ONE**
Feeling hungry?

Audrey Robinson wanted to help her children understand that even in America, children go to bed hungry. Audrey discovered *Uncle Willie and the Soup Kitchen* by DyAnne DiSalvo-Ryan. When she finished reading this children's book, she wanted to find a memorable way to help her children embrace a response to hunger, so she decided to read it to her youngest and let her two older girls read the book on their own.

As each child completed the book, Audrey began to have conversations about what it is like to be hungry. Blake, Payton, and Makaylee's first response after reading the book was, "People shouldn't be hungry. I am sad that kids are hungry." Blake, the youngest, kept asking *why*: "Why do people have to be poor? Why don't people have enough food?"

The discussion opened up his eyes to many other topics related to hunger. As Audrey spent time with each of her girls, both indicated how hard it would be to just be a kid, enjoying sports, playing with friends, or even school, if they were hungry. "If I had to take a test, all I would think about is that I am hungry," eight-year-old Payton told her mom. These girls realized the truth: When you are hungry, you can't focus on anything else.

"Our discussions then turned to what we could do for people who were hungry. I once thought hunger was an issue I couldn't impact, especially with my children, but now I realize that we can all go to Sam's Club and get things to donate to our food bank or summer lunch program. Even little children can get involved," Audrey shared.

I asked Audrey why she felt other parents should expose their children to the issue of hunger, and Audrey said, "It is important that children realize what is really going on in the world. Sometimes I think we protect them too much. They need to understand it as a child, so when they face it once they leave home, they'll know how to respond."

Here are some of the questions you might want to discuss with a child in your care, as Audrey did:

What does it feel like when you are hungry?

How does your body feel?

Take Action

Do you feel tired?

Do you feel like running, jumping, and playing?

Do you feel like reading and doing schoolwork?

What are you thinking about all the time?

About half of all children will spend a portion of their childhood in a single-parent home. [1]

More than one in eight children (13 percent) live in a neighborhood where the poverty rate is 30 percent or higher. [2]

Children of single parents are at higher risk of negative outcomes later in life, such as dropping out of school, becoming a teen parent, or going through a divorce in adulthood. [3]

10,887,000 children were living in families where the household head lack[ed] a high school diploma. [4]

Every year 27,000 foster care children turn 18 and "age out" of foster care, left to do life alone. [5]

PART THREE

ZERO ISOLATION

---

1. The process of being far away from other places, buildings, or people; remote[6]

2. The parent or caregiver consistently preventing the child from having normal social interactions with peers, family members, and adults.[7]

CHAPTER 7

ONE IS A LONELY NUMBER

It is necessary only for the good man to do
nothing for evil to triumph.
—EDMUND BURKE

IF YOU HAVE ANY DOUBT that living in isolation can have devastating effects on a person, Cora's story will dispel them. I first met her in the Wellspring Living Home, and I remember her always looking off in the distance, as though she either wasn't fully present or didn't want to be.

Little did I know that for this beautiful redhead in her thirties, with striking features and smooth olive skin, that vacancy behind her eyes was a reflection of the isolation she'd encountered for years growing up and into adulthood. Be prepared: her story is one of the tough ones. It's hard to read, but it happened and, as we've learned in working with people who have endured similar atrocities, it's not as uncommon as we'd like to think. Because she lived it herself, she's the best one to tell her story. Believe me, though: you'll want to see it through to the end, where there's beauty and hope.

Cora's Story:

I was born in 1982, in San Fernando Valley's North Hollywood neighborhood. My mother suffered from extreme schizophrenia, hearing voices and seeing visions almost constantly. My father, trying to get away from her, left me and my older sister behind to start a new life, far away from my mom's literal insanity.

It seemed we were always moving: not to a nicer, bigger house as some people expect to do, but always to a smaller, dingier, less safe place. My mom was deeply entrenched in the Church of Scientology, which shunned any sort of psychology or psychiatry, so she was determined not to receive any sort of help for her rapidly devolving mental state.

One of my favorite memories as a little girl was going to kindergarten in a crisp white blouse and a pink jumper that had tiny embroidered pansies along the hem. It was one of the few times in my life when I felt beautiful and safe.

A couple of years later when I was seven, my teacher asked to see my mother for a parent-teacher conference. During their meeting she dared to suggest that I might have OCD (obsessive-compulsive disorder) and that seeing a psychiatrist might help me focus. My mom freaked out and immediately pulled both me and my then-twelve-year-old sister out of school, dismissing my well-meaning teacher as a "suppressive person," which is Scientology's label for someone who can infect others with bad thoughts. Instead of learning in school, my sister and I were left at home from 7 a.m. to 10 p.m. to fend for ourselves, with strict instructions to stay inside our dismal apartment during school hours, so our neighbors and child protective officers wouldn't know we weren't in class.

My sister and I shared a room with our mom, while my younger brother and a male family friend slept on the living room sofas. The voices in my mother's head told her that she was in a relationship with a mysterious boyfriend, so when she was at home, she spent the majority of her time fantasizing vocally about her sexual relationship with a man who didn't exist. Her behavior was so shocking that I was afraid to bring friends over.

My sister, who was five years older than me, had to become more like a mother than a sister. When I was nine and she was fourteen, she found a twenty-seven-year-old boyfriend. My sister would bring me along to his place, and I'd play alone while they had sex in a back bedroom. I smoked pot for the first time when I was ten, using the high to mellow and numb my pain.

That same year, I enrolled in a private Scientology school with the financial help of a relative. Though I should've been at a higher grade level, grades didn't matter so much there. All of the school kids were in one big classroom, each studying a workbook "at their own pace." But I didn't get too much schooling, since my mom was getting scared for our safety because of the gang violence that surrounded our neighborhood, and she moved our family to Alaska, where her parents lived.

I was so eager to belong that I drank and drank. The next morning, I woke up in terrible pain.

I started public school in Anchorage and, though by age I was a fifth grader, I had the educational foundation of only a first grader. My teachers, not knowing my history, assumed I had a learning disability and put me into special education classes. I was afraid to tell the truth about my past, for fear that sharing my story would get my mom into trouble.

I was different than the other kids, constantly bullied and harassed. I made one friend and she invited me to spend time at her house. One night, her older brother was having a party outside around a bonfire. I ventured out and the boys invited me to join them, offering me beer and making me feel like one of their group. I was so eager to belong that I drank and drank. The next morning, I woke up in terrible pain and wearing only my underwear. I'd been raped by more than one of the brother's friends and there were Polaroid photos scattered around, chronicling the entire thing. I was embarrassed, but maybe shockingly, I also felt accepted in a way that I never had before.

Still in Anchorage, I started seventh grade and things really spiraled out of control. I had no care or supervision—my mom couldn't really even take care of herself. I dropped out of school and met a twenty-one-year-old guy named Danny. Even though I was only twelve, I told him I was fourteen, and he asked me to move in with him. My sister found out about it and told him the truth about my age, but his attitude was "Oh well, I love her, so I don't care how old she is." Memories of that time in my life are a blur, since in addition to having sex, we were doing drugs and drinking almost constantly. Even though my mom protested at first, she eventually relented and even bought us a set of pans as a housewarming present, which I took as an implied indication of her blessing.

Danny and I moved into another apartment, with a bunch of his friends as roommates. Violence was ever present there. I woke up one night to his roommates raping a homeless woman outside our room. I begged Danny to let me out to yell at them to stop, but he wouldn't, saying that they were drugged up and that I'd just get hurt. While he never hurt me with violence, Danny hurt my body by passing on to me a sexually transmitted disease. At just thirteen, I had to have part of my cervix scraped off to remove the dangerous cells.

Soon after, Danny and I broke up. I was left with an insatiable appetite for drugs, all kinds of them, and had become desensitized to offering my body to anyone who could give me something in return. At fifteen, I met an even older man, Tim, who treated me with more love and care than I'd ever known. He told me I was beautiful, that he treasured me and would protect me. Never mind the fact that he was married and twenty years older. He took me to sex shops to buy me provocative clothes and sky-high heels. We went to his friends' cocaine-fueled house parties (orgies, really) where everything was allowed. Tim never physically laid a hand on me, but he videotaped his friends'—mostly married couples—interactions with me. It took me years, well into my thirties in fact, to name Tim for what he was: my pimp.

He told me I was beautiful. Never mind the fact that he was married and twenty years older.

My life as a teen became one big cycle of drinking, doing drugs, stealing to find money for drugs and sex (sometimes as a means to get the drugs my body craved). One night, my "friends" wanted to go to an eighteen-and-over club. Since I was only sixteen, they left me outside to fend for myself. Some guys pulled up and asked if I wanted to party with them. I figured being in a warm car with beer was better than sitting in the dark and the cold. I was wrong. After a while of drinking, they got tired of me and pushed me out of the car and into a ditch. I woke up hours later with a concussion, shivering in the icy Alaska temperatures.

I was admitted to an inpatient program, where I proceeded to swallow a bunch of pills, trying to permanently end the pain I felt. That landed me in a mental institution for two weeks. During my stay in the hospital, they noticed that my walking was a little off and, for the first time, diagnosed me with scoliosis, a condition that could have been treated years before, had it been addressed medically. They fashioned a back brace, but to this day, I have trouble walking and can't move as effortlessly as I'd like. Looking back, I can see how neglect and isolation have shaped my life. My issue with scoliosis is a noticeable one, for sure. Another example: when I got lice as a child, rather than get the necessary medication to rid my head of bugs, my mom simply shaved off my hair—all of it.

The cumulative effect of these experiences and patterns has led to repeated cycles of destruction: bad relationships, dangerous drugs, and more than one suicide attempt. Even as I tell my story, I realize that as bad as it sounds, there was always a small grain of hope in my heart. I used to think, "One day I'll have the cute little house with the white picket fence and a couple of kids I can love and care for in all the ways I never was."

Of literally hundreds of times of having sex, I can say only maybe four were when I was sober. I would do anything to numb the pain that followed me everywhere in my waking hours and at night, even in my dreams. Through my relationships, I got pregnant twice, losing my babies both times. After all the mental and physical trauma I've endured, my body can't carry a child to term. The second pregnancy resulted in a rupture that sealed my fate of not being able to bear a biological child. I have angel wings tattooed on my left wrist, each symbolizing the babies I wanted to love but didn't have the chance to know.

She held my hand and looked into my eyes as my story came spilling out. I didn't hold anything back.

Throughout my twenties, I moved from Alaska to Georgia to Illinois to California, during which there were rapes, physical violence, and the ever-present substance abuse that dulled my senses and, I always hoped, my pain. Finally, I moved back to Georgia, where my sister's place was slightly less unsafe than where I'd been staying on the West Coast.

Not long after I arrived in the South, my sister and I for some reason went to church one day. That morning, a woman named Susan Norris could see that I was in a desperate place. She held my hand and looked into my eyes as my story came spilling out. I didn't hold anything back, but rather than shrinking away and making me feel like I was too damaged to care about, she said, "I have a friend who can help you." After the service, she sat with me as she called Mary Frances to see if they had any space available in the Wellspring Living Program.

In 2012, I went to Wellspring Living's Assessment Center, where I had the opportunity to rest, refocus, and acquire much-needed medical services, along with therapy and assessments to help me determine my next steps. For me, from the time I walked across the threshold of the Assessment Center, I wanted to go into the residential program that was just next door. I thought this was my chance to start over, but I was so nervous that it wouldn't happen because of my destructive past.

For the first time, I allowed myself to care about being accepted into something, desperate to grasp the recovery that the program offered. I got the news I was accepted and felt a rush of joy and an overwhelming wave of relief. I was so happy to be safe. I could finally stop running, for the first time since I was twelve years old. There I learned for the first time that God loves me and that there's hope for me.

Now twenty years later I breathed in and felt, instead of numbness, some clarity of a future for which I'd never dared to hope.

In the next step of the program, I participated in multiple classes and events that helped me see life through different eyes. I began to understand that everything that happened to me wasn't my fault. I looked at my life history, found patterns of destruction, and learned new coping mechanisms so I could address the pain and begin to heal. After months of intense therapy and activities that helped me begin to love myself, I moved into the Independent Living Program (ILP). It was like a dream, but I was so afraid I wouldn't be able to maintain this new way of life. I had a job at a factory, but I wanted more than a minimum-wage job. I was over thirty years old and had no real work experience, so how could I ever do anything else?

One evening, Laura Clark, a Wellspring Living board member, took the ILP ladies out to dinner and told us about a new opportunity. If we wanted, we would be able to continue to work at our present jobs, but a corporation I'd never heard of, Randstad US, would provide professional training so we might be able to move toward acquiring a living wage career position. It sounded too good to be true. In fact, I was pretty skeptical, but once I met the women who would be leading the program, I became encouraged. I began to look forward to Fridays to see what new things I would learn in the office.

I'd learned so much about my past and how to move forward in my recovery through Wellspring Living. While that is so necessary, what I lacked was the hope of a different future that would allow me to be a part of a company and become a valued employee. The first class was significant to me because I learned more about my personality and what kind of job matched my skills and interests. Each Friday became a treasure trove of discovery. Learning how to write a resume, role-playing for interviews, and researching potential employment opportunities was exhilarating! Maybe for the first time ever, I felt I had choices.

I was learning I could make friends who would connect with me for who I am, not for what they can take from me.

Two events stick out in my mind during this time as game changers for me. About halfway through the coursework on Fridays, Chandelle, one of the program leaders, told us that Randstad had decided that they would offer us a paid apprenticeship to practice what we'd learned. This news was such a boost! We would finally have something legitimate we could put on our resumes. I couldn't believe that they'd pay us to learn from them, and the pay was much more than I was presently making.

This exciting opportunity left us wondering how we would fit into a corporate environment, so the Wellspring/Randstad team decided to host an event to put our minds at ease. Laura invited us to her home, where she created a miniboutique with all kinds of career clothes, shoes, and accessories. We found out she'd been gathering these for months, and each of us left with huge shopping bags, filled with wonderful clothes for our upcoming apprenticeship. The next few Fridays were spent learning the corporate culture, giving us each confidence to enter the next chapter professionally. I began to be truly hopeful I wouldn't be alone anymore. Now I would be a part of a team at work. My mentors would be beside me to cheer me on. I was learning I could make friends who would connect with me for who I am, not for what they can take from me.

It's like a dream I've always had, but never believed was possible.

As Cora made that final statement, she and I both had tears in our eyes, because now, a year later, what she wished was becoming a reality. Cora is splitting her time between two locations, developing valuable onboarding processes for the company. She's made some amazing, supportive friends, and her mentors from Wellspring Living are never far from her. As she rose to leave to meet a friend for dinner, Cora pulled something out of her purse to show me. There, on a creamy white card, in bold letters, was her name. "See, I even have a business card!" She beamed, her smile and bright, clear eyes radiating as only someone who has true hope can.

REACT

How do you feel after reading Cora's story? Angry for the abuse and neglect she suffered? Amazed that someone with such a tough background could be reached, helped, and changed? Have you heard of others whose situation seems hopeless? Have you ever felt hopeless yourself?

CHAPTER 8

ONE LIFE-GIVING GIFT

I am only one, but I am still one. I cannot
do everything, but I can still do something.
And, because I cannot do everything, I will not
refuse to do the something I can do.
—EDWARD EVERETT HALE, AUTHOR OF
THE MAN WITHOUT A COUNTRY

Rick's Story:

My name's Richard, but everyone calls me Rick. I was born in 1954 at Georgia Baptist Hospital in Atlanta, the only child of my mom, who was an extreme alcoholic. My biological dad wasn't ever in the picture but there were plenty of men in my life. You see, I had seven stepfathers (or at least I assumed they were: they lived with us and acted "married" to my mom) by the time I was twelve years old. We moved a lot, and as a result, I went to eight different elementary schools, scattered throughout the city's slums.

I was sad a lot of the time. Nothing in my life was stable or safe. My mom was totally different when she was drinking. In her sober moments, she was very nice, but totally incompetent and unequipped to be a parent. But when she was drinking, she was mean-spirited, abusive, and completely irrational.

From some of my earliest memories, I'd seen things that I now realize children should never have to see. I saw my mom attack one of her husbands with a broken liquor bottle, slicing into an artery. Our living room looked like the scene of a massacre —fresh blood was everywhere. I'm not sure how, but he lived. The hospital stitched him up and sent him home to us. Another time, I watched from the car as my mom was beaten up on the front porch of our house. All I could think was, *Well, she probably deserved it.* The isolation I felt made it easiest for me to detach completely.

As we moved from one housing project to another, I quickly learned that fighting was a fast way to earn the respect of my new peers and avoid being bullied. I was a scrappy but not a particularly large child. I usually didn't ask for a fight but was taught not to run from one either. I also learned how to be cunning. One time, a kid two grades older wanted to fight me. I lied and told him I didn't want to fight and, while he stood there laughing at me, I punched him square in the nose, knocking him to the ground. I climbed on top of him, pummeling him until he ran off. No one ever messed with me at that school again.

My mother used to leave me alone for hours, sometimes days, at a time. Oddly, as long as there was food in the cupboard, I almost felt safer when she wasn't there. At least on my own I knew what to expect. When she was around, she embarrassed me all the time. Once we were driving past a Greyhound bus station and she said she had to use the bathroom. Instead of parking and going inside to find a restroom, she got out, hiked up her dress and began peeing right on the sidewalk. The next day, when she'd sobered up, she thought I was lying when I told her what she'd done. The police were often called to our house, and one time they had to drag her naked out to the paddy wagon. I was mortified and hid in my room, relieved to just have some peace while she was in jail.

I felt pretty sure I didn't matter to anyone. How awful is that?

There were a few things I knew innately: I should try to do well in school, since that could be important in the future, so I wouldn't end up like my mom and the men in our lives. I learned how to make friends quickly. And I needed money, since I saw that money was power and would be my ticket out of this kind of life.

I was nothing if not industrious. In the shadow of Georgia Tech University, I started scalping tickets when I was only ten. I bagged groceries at the local Joy Supermarket. I took up a paper route, and on Friday nights, I'd walk downtown to the Peach Bowl Race Track, selling popcorn, peanuts, and Cracker Jacks. It was certainly no place for a kid, but there was no one to tell me not to go or what to do. One of the saddest days of my life was when at eleven, I won the all-star player award in my Little League baseball league at Atlantic Steel. No one was there to see it—not my mom, not any of my stepfathers, and certainly not my real dad, who I didn't know. I felt pretty sure I didn't matter to anyone. How awful is that?

Christmases were always a big deal in our house. No matter how bad things were, my mom always managed to pull together great gifts, though often getting wasted the night before and using the presents as a sort of peace offering to soothe her guilt. One year, I had a really good Christmas, complete with every toy I wanted and even a really terrific bike. It was a kid's dream: I even threw up, I was so happy. When I found out that some of my friends down the block hadn't gotten any gifts, I gave away some of my loot. My mom beat me hard that day for doing that.

When I was twelve, we went to a party with relatives in Marietta, a northern suburb of Atlanta. My mom was wasted and it always scared me when I had to ride with her when she was drunk. Everyone else at the party was wasted too, so I took the keys away and, even though my feet barely reached the pedals, what should have been a twenty-minute drive on the interstate home took me hours to drive on the back roads that night.

They couldn't believe that I could have reached thirteen and completely slipped through the cracks for so long.

On my thirteenth birthday, we visited my uncle's house in Stone Mountain, another Atlanta suburb, and the situation repeated itself almost exactly. Only this time, I told my Uncle Bubba that I wasn't leaving with my mom. I was sick and tired of being terrified. I'd had enough. He offered to let me stay with him that night while my mom took her life and anyone else's she encountered on the road in her hands as she drove home drunk. Uncle Bubba was a paraplegic, so it wasn't feasible for me to stay with him long-term, even though we had a good relationship and I knew he loved me. Instead, he used the lion's share of his disability check to call a taxi to take me to child welfare services. He dropped me off and said, "Good luck!"

Initially, the child welfare caseworkers assumed

I'd been in trouble and made a move to put me in a juvenile correctional center. Why else would I have found myself "kicked out of my home"? I told them it wasn't true. My mom was just unfit to take care of me. They were baffled because they couldn't believe that I could have reached thirteen and completely slipped through the cracks for so long. In fact, no one even knew I needed help. Soon enough, they found out my story was true and took steps to place me into a temporary home to get me acclimated to the system. Mom didn't fight it, knowing she couldn't take care of me herself.

I was placed in a temporary home for ninety days, even though I was only supposed to stay for thirty. Then I went for an interview with the Prices, a nice, stable family with four children of their own and a two-year-old foster child. When they took me in, I thought I'd hit the jackpot. They had a nice, five-bedroom home. They held hands and prayed before dinner each night, Mr. Price saying, "Thank you, Lord, for giving us our children to love." It was hard to get used to, hearing my name in that list. All of this seemed so strange to me; I just couldn't figure it out. All of us kids went to a Christian summer camp that year, and I met a coach who was going to be the principal of a new private school that the community was putting together. He asked the Prices if I could come and play basketball, but they said no, because they'd promised their daughter that she could go first. I did what seemed most natural to me when I felt rejected. I eventually ran away.

When the social workers found me, they put me back with my mom, but that only lasted for a few months. It just didn't work, particularly after I'd seen what a functioning family looked like. My only other option was the Methodist Children's Home, an orphanage. There were ten cabins, five for girls and five for boys, each with a young married couple who served as cottage parents. Since many of the kids were antisocial, I became a bit of a leader there, organizing ball games and such. I actually liked it there, since it was stable and predictable.

The one time of year that was particularly hard for me, though, was Christmas. Most of the kids would go spend the holiday with whatever extended family they had, even if it was a distant aunt or grandparent, but I didn't want to see my mom, knowing nothing good was likely to come out of it. The halls of my dorm were silent on that chilly Christmas Eve night. I was fourteen and I cried myself to sleep, certain that no one would remember me for Christmas, feeling as alone and isolated as I could remember.

The next morning, I woke up and through my tear-reddened eyes, I saw an oversized white envelope underneath the door with my name on it, scrawled in an unfamiliar handwriting. I padded over in my stocking feet and picked it up, tearing into it. Out fell a crisp, $100 bill and a simple note that said, "Merry Christmas from an anonymous donor." I'd never seen so much money! And I wondered: why would someone who doesn't even know me care enough to give me such an extravagant gift? Here I was abandoned by my whole family, yet someone who didn't even know me cared enough to give me this extravagant gift. It was a brand of giving I'd never seen before.

I wondered: why would someone who doesn't even know me care enough to give me such an extravagant gift?

I went to the electronics store and bought myself a record player for $50, the most money I'd spent on any one item, ever, and I tucked the other $50 in change back into my pocket. When the guys came back from the holiday, they showed me their "loot"—baseball gloves, footballs, G.I. Joes. But, for five of the guys, they didn't have anything to show. I remembered my $50 and rushed back to the store to purchase five transistor radios. As I gave them to my friends, all of them were thrilled, save one: the boy across the hall took the radio with downcast eyes and just a mumbled "Thanks." I didn't understand. Maybe he didn't like the radio. Then I remembered the Prices. They'd tried to show me the love of a family, the kind of familial love I'd never known and didn't know how to accept. It started to click into place for me that I didn't have to go it alone all the time.

I don't know how she found me, but a year later, Bobbi Jean Price (my "sister") wrote me and invited me to join them for Thanksgiving dinner. I accepted, and right after Mr. Price said grace, Bobbi Jean blurted out, "We should ask Rick to come back to live with us!" Everyone, including me, was shocked. Her words broke the ice, though, and soon after, I was back living with them, isolated no longer, but part of a true family. It was 1970, in my junior year of high school. I did play baseball at that private school and graduated, on time and with honors.

I went on to put myself through college, start a business, and became the dad of three amazing kids. I've been far from a perfect parent, but my kids will tell you that they were always my top priority and they never felt abandoned. I'm really proud of that. I've tried for years to find the person who gave me that life-changing gift, but there's no record or paper trail. It wasn't the amount of money, but the generosity that lifted me out of isolation and caused me to begin to change my thinking. I'm so grateful that someone stepped outside of himself to include me. It spoke to my young heart and told me I mattered, and it may well have changed the trajectory of my life.

More than four decades later, that little boy has grown into a generous man. Each Christmas, he writes an abbreviated version of his story on a note, wrapped around a $100 bill, which he gives to children without families, children like he once was, who have experienced the ache of isolation and abandonment.

You never know who a child will grow up to be. Often, they only need a chance—someone or a group of "someones"—to come alongside them and tell them, "You matter. I'm here for you. You have so much potential." The little boy who told this story grew up to be Rick Jackson, a successful businessman and the CEO of Jackson Healthcare, one of the largest private healthcare staffing agencies in the United States, serving more than five million patients nationwide. Rick is father to three grown children and a still-growing group of grandchildren. He sits on the board of more than a half dozen nonprofit organizations, many of which he supports through his own Jackson Family Foundation.

He's doing tremendous good in the world, across various charitable organizations, but his real passion is serving foster children, a cause he understands intimately. In 2009, he started FaithBridge Foster Care in Georgia, a faith-based organization that seeks to change the way America does foster care by mobilizing, organizing, and equipping local churches to solve their community's foster care crisis. Through this model, FaithBridge provides unparalleled support to foster and birth families through a "community of care" model. In this structure, they help find resources like tutoring, mentoring, babysitting, transportation, and other assistance as needed. It's really making a difference for these families.

Rick is a modest man, who doesn't easily admit the great work he has accomplished. He is allowing the pain of his past to bring hope to thousands of children in Georgia and beyond. Rick is an expert on what isolated children have experienced, and keenly understands what is needed to move a child from isolation to a caring community.

REACT

Have you ever been given an anonymous gift? What were the circumstances and the impact? Have you ever given someone a significant gift—or note—anonymously?

CHAPTER 9

ONE SAFE PLACE

It is the greatest of all mistakes to do nothing because you can only do little—do what you can.
—SYDNEY SMITH

ISOLATED CHILDREN do not all look the same. They may not be in foster care or experiencing a dangerous home life. They can be children living in a community that simply needs more support or in a family that cannot provide adequate supervision because of long work hours. This dilemma is one many families face daily. Even with parents' best intentions, children can find themselves isolated.

Some of the greatest strides forward can be born out of need or tragedy. That's how the start of a truly effective program in my hometown began. It was a dark time in Atlanta from 1979 to 1981, when twenty-eight African-American children, adolescents, and adults were murdered. Beginning the summer of 1979, two fourteen-year-old boys disappeared just four days apart and were found murdered. A little more than a month later, another adolescent boy took his 10-speed bike to go to the bank for his mother and was never seen alive again. The panic in the city continued to build as a nine-year-old boy offered to run an errand for an elderly neighbor and was found strangled in an abandoned elementary school lot two weeks later. Parents were terrified. Children who had enjoyed the innocence and freedom to play outdoors were afraid even to walk down the street in broad daylight. Friends became suspects while there was a phantom killer on the loose.

Then in spring of 1980, a young black girl was found raped, strangled, and tied to a tree. Her parents' hearts broke, and the community, even those who didn't know this little girl, supported the family by attending her funeral.

In June, a seven-year-old girl was abducted, taken right from her own home, finally prompting the FBI to get involved. Of course, everyone feared the worst. The mystery had governmental officials and police perplexed. The community educated their children about safety, but after twelve children were abducted, parents couldn't remain quiet any longer.

The entire community took to searching the area surrounding where the children were abducted. When the abducted girl was found dead by the search party, massive outrage resulted. Parents begged the government to find the perpetrator and ensure the safety of their children. Atlanta's burgeoning tourism business slowed to a crawl in the wake of the murders, and many conventions were moved to venues outside of Atlanta. Palpable terror prevailed, but no solutions were in sight.

The horrific crime spree lasted twenty-two months, during which victims were found strangled, shot, and bludgeoned to death. It's hard to even fathom the distrust and suffocating fear in the city, like wearing a wool coat and scarf in the heat of summer. An arrest was eventually made in this case.

In the midst of this turmoil, Eston Hood, a then-twenty-four-year-old employee of the YMCA in Southwest Atlanta, felt he had to do something proactive. In his own words, Eston shares his quest to find a solution that would help keep children safe.

Eston's Story:

When I found out these cases involved school-aged children, I was very concerned. With my work at the Y, I feared that some of *my* kids could go missing. After all, I was leading programs in the exact area where the murders had taken place. At that time in Atlanta, schools completely shut down at the end of the school day, leaving children to fend for themselves until their parents could come home from work. It seemed like our boys and girls were prey to anyone who might want to harm them. This was just not acceptable, so I thought, *Why not see if there is any way we can work alongside schools to provide a safety net for our children?* They were good kids, smart kids. They just needed a safe place.

I met with Atlanta school officials to discuss keeping the schools open until 6:00 p.m. and allowing the YMCA to provide the supervision and programming after the official school day ended. Dr. Crabb, the superintendent of Atlanta schools at that time, was on our corporate board, so he became my first point of contact to expound upon my idea. Influential Atlantans, including Ambassador Andrew Young, Milton Jones, Mayor Maynard Jackson, Michael Lomax, and Marvin Arrington, all had children who participated in the programs I ran at the Southwest YMCA, and they all gave their strong support. Everyone wanted to find a way to keep children safe, so we pulled together to initiate the program. We shared the responsibilities: the schools provided the facilities and the YMCA provided the program.

We began with the Atlanta City Schools, and then later expanded to surrounding metro counties including Fulton, DeKalb, and then Clayton. There was a wonderful outpouring of support for the YMCA because we were willing to help parents be assured of their children's safety. It started out with enrichment and recreational services, and later expanded to include academic services.

The dynamic and much-needed program began thirty-five years ago with an energetic twentysomething employee. Now that same employee, Eston Hood, is the COO of the Metro Atlanta YMCA, and he continues to impact children who need a safe place while parents are at work.

One of the YMCAs that has a particularly strong before- *and* after-school program is in Norcross, Georgia. Just like Eston, Mark Thornell, executive director of the Fowler YMCA, realized the tremendous value in working alongside local schools and parents to ensure safe care of children, rather than creating a separate program on his own. Pinckneyville Middle School is just a few blocks from the Fowler YMCA, so it seemed a natural opportunity to partner together for a common goal of creating a safe, fun place for middle schoolers, who would most likely otherwise go home to an empty home or apartment.

In collaboration with the school's principal and advisors, a robust program was designed to provide after-school enrichment, leadership development, homework assistance, and fitness. The YMCA staff engages teachers to participate and help identify children who actually require extra support. The dire need for the safety provided in the Y's program was highlighted by tragedy recently, when two students living in a nearby low-income apartment complex lost their lives during the hours between when school let out and when their parents arrived home from work. While the students who died (one was murdered and the other committed suicide) were not participants in the program, the question of whether access to positive influences, role models, and continuing education might have made a difference for these two students still plagues Mark's mind.

As proactive YMCA leaders began to look for an even more holistic approach to creating safety and positive influences for youth, to further combat the ever-present danger of isolation, it became clear that before-school programs were also needed. Many parents, trying to make ends meet, have to leave for work long before school starts, so the YMCA has become a place where students can come as early as 6:00 a.m. during the week. It's a safe place to interact with their peers, receive homework help, and get ready to start a day of learning.

The danger of isolation creeping into a child's or teen's life doesn't only happen during the school year.

The danger of isolation creeping into a child's or teen's life doesn't only happen during the school year, so one of the YMCA's programs that becomes a safe place is summer camp. In talking with Mark and one of his youth leaders, Jen Young, I was introduced to Jonathan.

He's a high school student who is a part of the YMCA Leaders in Training, an extension of camp that allows older campers to help lead and mentor younger participants.

Jonathan and his mom have given permission to tell his story of how the Y has positively impacted his life. Here's a glimpse of his application to L.I.T., where he writes, "My interest in this program is rooted in the fact that I have been participating in summer camp since I was four years old. I believe this job will help me obtain great leadership skills, preparing me for a great job one day. My hopes are to get useful skills so I can improve myself and use them for future opportunities."

Those words seem to indicate a confident fourteen-year-old, but Jonathan's story didn't begin that way. Listen as this tall, lanky high schooler describes his struggles.

Jonathan's Story:

I have a cholesteatoma that would sometimes wrap around my eardrum and facial tissue. I had to have two surgeries a year to take the tissue out, and at age twelve, the growth finally stopped. Due to this and the surgeries, I had an 80 percent hearing loss in my left ear. It affected my speech, which means I've been seeing a speech therapist since I was four years old. My hearing loss and speech impediment brought challenges in school. I also had to deal with bullying from my peers. As an athlete, I struggled with hearing on the field, so it was difficult to take accurate direction from my coaches.

I overcame classroom challenges by sitting in the front, having notes written by peers, and asking people to speak to me on my right side. For lacrosse, I work to be a great athlete, so it is not noticeable that I have a hearing loss or am considered disabled. The YMCA taught me to treat others kindly, even when I am not treated kindly. The YMCA gave me support so I never felt left out. When I'm feeling overwhelmed, my counselors have always listened and cared.

Jonathan recognized that Jen and her staff have supported him as he grew through his challenges to redirect and build into his character. Having a safe place at the YMCA to experience care, refine his natural leadership qualities, and become a skilled athlete were vital to Jonathan's development, one who is equipped to accomplish whatever he desires in life, be it college, a career, and beyond.

Wess Stafford, another compassionate advocate for children and author of *Just a Minute* wrote, "With each child you encounter, you have the power and opportunity to build up . . . or, sadly, to tear down. A life can be literally launched

> **Giving multiple intentional "minutes" to children is what makes the cumulative difference.**

with as little as a single word, an uplifting comment, a well-timed hug, a tender prayer, a compliment, the holding of a frightened hand, or the gentle wiping of a tear—all in just a minute!"[8]

Before I dug deeper, my impression of the YMCA's work with children was limited to a place for services from swim lessons and gymnastics, and even childcare while moms exercise. However, I'm grateful to have learned about how much more they offer: they truly create a place of safety and consistent care in the community. Their positive results are big: 86 percent of students in the low-income summer program had a significant increase in reading skills, 75 percent of them said they have a positive view of learning, and a whopping 94 percent identified at least one adult staff member they could point to as a positive role model. That kind of encouragement, camaraderie, and accountability is priceless.

Of course, the numbers themselves are encouraging, but the one-to-one, daily dedication of YMCA staff members and volunteers giving multiple intentional "minutes" to children is what makes the cumulative difference. From wiping tears after a fall to helping navigate a difficult math concept to celebrating a win on the basketball court, children are learning life lessons with caring adults. Like Jonathan, many children are finding a safe place to fail and succeed—to be kids. There are 2,686 YMCAs across the United States, which serve 21 million people each year, including nearly 10 million children ages seventeen and under, but there are also conscientious educators, volunteer sports coaches, etc., who pour into the lives of children in their communities who desperately need a positive influence to stave off the risks that come from isolation.

Every positive interaction, no matter how small, is making an immeasurable impact.

REACT

Who were some positive role models you remember? Who are some children you could have an impact on with "just a minute" efforts as Wess Stafford mentions?

CHAPTER 10

ONE OPEN DOOR

The love of a foster mother for her charge
appears absolutely irrational.
—WINSTON CHURCHILL

PAM PARISH has a beautiful family, but it doesn't look like mine, and I can almost guarantee it doesn't look like yours either. When I saw her last, she showed me a photo of "her girls," the seven young women who call her Mom, a multicultural group, all within five years of age of one another.

You see, Pam and her husband, Steve, had one biological daughter, born in 1995. After a number of medical challenges and close calls, they weren't able to give Kristan a sibling, something each of them desperately wanted. They thought they might add another child to their family through international adoption.

In 2006, shortly after moving to Atlanta from Raleigh, North Carolina, Pam watched a Public Broadcasting documentary on Heart Gallery of America, a national nonprofit organization that pairs volunteer photographers and videographers with foster children in the United States who are in need of forever homes. They shoot photos and videos that showcase these precious kids' unique personalities, in hopes of sparking the interest of the right family.

The program pierced Pam's heart and she couldn't get it out of her mind. Shortly thereafter, she and Steve signed up to take the state's foster care certification course, IMPACT, through a private agency. During the informative class, their hearts broke further as they learned how children who've been removed from their biological parents' homes are placed into foster care while their parents work on a case plan to regain custody. For roughly a quarter of the children, their parents will never complete the required steps and the state moves to permanently terminate parental rights through the courts, effectively becoming the "parent" of the child.

Devastatingly, there are thousands upon thousands of children across the country who are wards of the state. And, as you might expect, the older the children are, the smaller their chances of actually being adopted into a family that will love them their whole lives.

By the spring of 2007, with foster care and adoption training completed, the Parishes joined the ranks of hundreds of other preadoptive parents in the difficult in-between stage of waiting for a child who would become a forever part of their family.

As they waited, they immersed themselves in their new community and city, but the thought of adding a child to their family was never far from Pam's mind. Fortunately, Steve and their daughter Kristan were equally excited about a new family member. Blonde-haired, blue-eyed, eleven-year-old Kristan especially eagerly anticipated her new sister's arrival, meticulously dividing her toys, dolls, and stuffed animals between her room and the one next door.

HEATHER

In July of 2007, a photo of a spunky eleven-year-old popped up on Pam's online adoption registry. Heather had a big personality and an even bigger chip on her shoulder about the notion of being adopted.

She wanted no part of it. Who could blame her? She'd been in foster care since she was just six years old, with two adoptive placements that had fallen through at the last minute. She was used to having people come into her life, say they loved her and would adopt her, only to have those same people send her back when her behavior became challenging. Not surprisingly, she moved into the Parish family convinced that they weren't going to stick it out, and she even tried to speed up the process by letting her "difficult side" hang out early on. She was an expert in pushing the buttons that would drive her prospective parents away, but Pam and Steve were committed to loving her no matter what, just as they did their own flesh-and-blood child.

The Parishes' dreams of an idyllic life as a family of four quickly got turned upside down as reality set in. All of the things that they took for granted as "normal"—the food they ate, the activities they enjoyed doing as recreation, their habits at home—weren't normal for Heather, and everything felt like an uphill battle. In addition, Heather and Kristan couldn't attend the same

They only intended to adopt one child.

school. Though they were the same age and should have been in the same grade, they were in vastly different stages academically. Due to the instability in Heather's life, she was behind in almost every subject, pulling in Ds and sometimes Fs. The public school Kristan attended wanted to put Heather in special needs classes, and the Parishes knew that once she was labeled as a special needs student, she might never catch up with her peers. Heather was extremely bright; she just needed help gaining momentum.

So, with Heather's input, they enrolled her in a private school with smaller class sizes and rigorous academic standards. That first year, she barely passed, but she developed solid academic habits that would serve her well for the rest of her school days. As Heather came to know and trust that there was nothing she could do that would make her new family love her any less, she blossomed and flourished, resting in the knowledge that she'd found her forever home.

"We didn't start the journey into foster care or adoption because we wanted a big family or even because we wanted to give a child with no family a home," Pam explains. "Really, we started the journey because we wanted to add another daughter to our family and Kristan had always wanted a sister. We intended to be a 'one and done' adoptive family."

It's sort of comical, knowing what I know now about the Parishes, that they only intended to adopt one child. In fact, Pam will tell you that their second adoption came as a total surprise to her. After going through the challenges and joys of adding Heather to their family, Pam became more and more involved in their Atlanta-based adoption agency, eventually teaching IMPACT as a state-certified trainer for prospective foster and adoptive families.

KELSEY

One of the couples attending her IMPACT course shared their struggles with their fifteen-year-old foster-to-adopt daughter. It became apparent that they were heading toward a disruption—the term used in the system when a family asks for a child to be removed from their home. Pam casually shared the heartbreaking story of this teen, Kelsey, over the course of a conversation with Steve, before moving on to share other parts of her day. Steve couldn't let it go; he abruptly said, "Call the caseworker and tell her we'll take Kelsey. No one should have to live without a family."

Kelsey joined the Parish family two weeks later, the same day she met them for the first time. She arrived on the doorstep with a garbage bag of her few belongings; she had been in and out of foster care since she was eight. She had an ultra go-with-the-flow attitude, and Pam assumed that this adoption would run smoothly and easily. Soon after the paperwork was finalized in 2009, Pam began to realize that, particularly with adoptions, when something looked too easy, it probably was.

Pam puts it like this:

"In foster care and adoption, there's something very beautiful and broken in safety. It's more than just being in an environment where you're no longer abused or neglected. The deeper part, the one of belonging, is much more personal, risky and difficult. It's the safety of having to allow those inner thoughts—fears, worries, memories, hopes, dreams and ideas—out into the open space in a relationship and to trust that the other person is going to handle them with care. After all, those things represent you, your very heart. It's our human nature to compare the worst of ourselves against the best of others, and in that game, we all come out losers. How much more so in a sixteen-year-old's mind?"

You see, belonging was so much more difficult for Kelsey than Pam and Steve knew, and from her broken sense of identity, the need to call the shots in her own life, and the fear of being seen, she ran. One day, she just didn't come home from school; Kelsey had cleaned out her bank account and ditched her phone. Steve and Pam found her that first time, but the cycle repeated itself time and time again. She'd run, they'd find her, and they'd assure her that she was loved, accepted, and wanted. Things would be fine for a short time and then she'd run again. The last time, she ran into the near-clutches of a trafficker. It was then that Pam called me, desperate for Kelsey to enter the safety and treatment at Wellspring Living.

In October 2010, Pam sat with friends and strangers around a table, stuffing envelopes for the premier of *The Candy Shop*, a short film that used an allegorical tale to tell about the issue of domestic minor sex trafficking set in Atlanta. One of the women there was in the process of finalizing the adoption of elementary-aged siblings from foster care when someone asked her why she and her husband wouldn't just enjoy being empty nesters. She recited James 1:27 from the Bible ("Religion that God our Father accepts as pure and faultless is this: to look after orphans and widows in their distress") but added with a laugh that the Bible neglects to mention anything about when it's time to retire.

The thought haunted Pam and pushed her to open her mind and heart to others who needed a forever family.

KATYA

In February 2011, the Parishes got a phone call that changed everything. Ashley, a coworker of Pam's at the church, told her a story of Gregg, a missionary friend, who served in Ukraine. They discovered an eighteen-year-old girl who was at high risk of being trafficked, and actually, in all likelihood had already been sold ahead of her US citizenship being renounced. She'd been an orphan in Ukraine from infancy to age twelve, when a couple in Georgia had adopted her. After moving to the States, the adoptive father abused her mercilessly. At eighteen, she shared about the abuse with her adoptive mother, who refused to believe her. Instead of protecting or helping the teen, the woman bought her a one-way ticket back to her country of origin. On his first meeting with her after she had been back in Ukraine for a few months, Gregg, the missionary, noticed how strong her English skills were, spoken with a Southern accent to boot, and suspected that the girl had spent a good amount of time in the States. He and his team took swift action to find safety for her.

From the first telling of the incredibly sad story, Pam and Steve knew this girl was their daughter. After flying back to the States, Katya met the Parishes, who offered her a home and a family. After all she'd been through—adoption, abuse, being sent away and flying back to the United States after four months in Eastern Europe—she accepted the offer. "I don't know that I would've had the courage to say yes, to try again if I'd been through what she had, yet Katya did and I deeply admire her for it," Pam says as she talks fondly of her Ukrainian daughter.

There's something about unconditional love, especially when you've never had it, that feels like you're standing atop a 150-foot bungee drop, with an impossibly thin cord attached and an instructor telling you to jump. It's easier to trust what you know, even if what you know can devastate you.

Katya's life at the Parishes' was a bit like that. Until moving in, there had never been someone whose love she hadn't had to work for, perform for, or chase after. Even though their love was freely given, she didn't know how to receive it, so she fought. Pam remembers, "During one pretty significant fight, I grabbed her and held on tight and said, 'Katya, I will fight for you and with you for the rest of your life because I believe in you and love you. One day, you're going to do something amazing, and I will be your biggest cheerleader.'" Day by day, Katya has opened her heart and embraced being part of a family that loves her, blossoming into a woman of strength and courage.

ELIZABETH

Not long after Katya was settling in as a Parish girl, Pam's phone rang. It was nearly midnight, in May of 2012. On the other end of the phone were Dennis and Colleen Rouse, the leaders of the church where Pam and Steve worked, telling her of a girl who showed up on their doorstep needing help. She'd fled her home a few weeks earlier, after a family member pulled a knife—putting a punctuation mark on a string of abusive incidents. At seventeen, Elizabeth wasn't old enough to be on her own, but she couldn't go back home. The pastors were heading out of town and needed a safe connection to make sure she was taken care of. Pam laughs as she recounts the conversation in which Dennis said, "We're not looking for you to adopt her, just to make sure she has a safe place to be for a little while." Yeah, right.

They offered her a forever place in their family.

Pam agreed to take her shopping and to talk with her about a plan for her future, making sure she had a phone and a place to stay, counseling Elizabeth in a way that Pam was uniquely qualified to do, given her experience with her other girls. Over the next few months, she got to know this spunky, spirited, witty young Korean woman, ferrying her to doctor's and dentist's appointments and lunch dates, each time it seemed, picking her up from a different friend's house where she happened to be sleeping at the time.

Over the summer months, the Parishes included Elizabeth in family plans, hoping to involve her in activities that were fun and lighthearted. However, over time, Pam began to notice a veneer of depression and exhaustion settling over Elizabeth. She asked to meet and, over coffee, Pam's suspicions were confirmed. In a flood of tears, Elizabeth poured out her fears, doubts, and sadness. "I'll never forget her makeup-smeared, worn-out face as she talked with such hopelessness about her future," Pam remembers. "It broke my heart in a million pieces." It became evident that, more than anything, she needed family and stability. She needed to know that she belonged and that someone would always be there for her. Sitting over breakfast, Pam offered her just that—a forever place in their family.

SEARA

The following summer in June 2013, Katya (who had been away studying at a leadership program at a ministry academy) asked if she could talk with her parents when they returned from work. She told them about a girl in her school who was there on scholarship, but who would be homeless after the school year ended. Seara (pronounced "Sarah") had endured a lifetime of verbal, mental, and physical abuse, which drove her to run shortly after she turned eighteen and before she was to graduate high school. The story tugged at Pam's heartstrings, of course, but they were running out of room. She says, "I'll never forget my husband's words as we were discussing the decision to invite her into our family. He said, 'It doesn't matter to me if all we have is a corner to sleep in, having a corner and family to support you is better than having no one.' I'm telling you, he is my hero."

Seara came into the Parish family without any form of ID, no knowledge of her birth mother, and contact with her birth father that could be described as sparse, at best. Everyone who had cared for her up to that point in her life had made her feel like a burden, an extra mouth to feed and a problem that they didn't ask for and didn't really want. The only way out of that and into a life of wholeness is courage and determination, and Seara has determination in spades. She's fiercely loyal to those she loves and driven to carve out a life for herself that includes giving back to others along the way.

CHARLIE

Pam laughed out loud when I asked her if she plans to adopt again. "I stopped saying that our family is complete," she says. It's a good thing, because a young woman named Charlie would've proved her wrong. Instead of looking toward her eighteenth birthday with anticipation of independence and adulthood, Charlie looked at the date with a sickening mixture of dread and anxiety. Why? Her eighteenth birthday represented a deadline. It was the day she had to move into a homeless shelter or find a program that would accept her.

Charlie's foster family made the situation very clear: "You're not staying here. You're responsible for finding a new place to live. If you haven't found a new place by your birthday, we will drop you off at the nearest homeless shelter."

So her teachers and school administrators emailed, called, and texted just about everyone they could think of. Pam and Steve got the email just one day before the deadline—her birthday—so time was short. It was the middle of her senior year of high school, so she was about to have to cut her education short, leave school, and figure out life on her own. The Parishes contacted the teacher who'd sent the email and agreed to meet the next day. "Surrounded by teachers and administrators, we met Charlie in an office of her high school." Pam remembers, "She cried. We cried. Teachers, the principal, and school nurses cried."

You know what happened, of course. Charlie is now a part of the Parish family. She has a solid family foundation to help her transition into her future: a mom, a dad, and siblings who will always be involved in her life, rooting for her along the way. "It terrifies me to think about what could have happened to our precious daughter if we hadn't said yes," Pam says.

The reality of what teens coming out of foster care face is bleak. Young adults between the ages of eighteen to twenty-four are particularly vulnerable to homelessness. At any given time, there are more than 55,000 homeless young adults in the United States alone, with 122,000 experiencing at least a period of "transitional" homelessness annually. Each year 27,000 children turn eighteen and age out of foster care. Left alone to do life alone—without a caring family to walk beside them—the statistics are grim.[9] Only 4 percent will go on to complete a four-year college degree (compared to 36 percent of the general population). One in five will be homeless after eighteen. Only half will be employed full-time by age twenty-four. Seventy-one percent of young women will be pregnant by age twenty-one. By age twenty-four, 60 percent of young men will have been incarcerated. Perhaps worst of all, 70 percent of all sex trafficking victims were former foster children.[10]

Struck by the very real need to combat the overwhelming realities and aware that her home could only be so big, in 2014 Pam launched Connection Homes, a nonprofit that helps connect young adults without family support with families who will love them forever. The idea is to raise up other families, so these young adults will be able to reach their potential within the security and support of a real family.

Heather, who struggled so much initially with school, has graduated with honors from high school and is going on to pursue a college degree as a special-needs teacher. Kelsey is an amazing mom of four beautiful children. Katya is working at a job she loves and considering pursuing an education in political science, a pathway that will allow her to help people and take part in influencing international adoption policy. Elizabeth is working full-time and was recently promoted to a management position while also enrolled in college. Seara married the love of her life, Tyree, and is on the staff of Connection Homes, helping pave the way for other young adults to find forever families. Charlie has graduated from high school and is going on to pursue a college degree.

Kristan is enrolled in college and is on staff at the church her mom and dad work for. The journey of her family hasn't been easy for her, and both she and her parents are quick to admit that a lot of mistakes were made along the way in their relationship. Yet through it all, she remains grateful to have her sisters to share life with and her parents as role models of compassion and grace.

Not everyone is called to adopt or foster. I would go so far as to say that if it's not something that you feel strongly about doing, you shouldn't. It's one of the hardest experiences a family can go through, and without the assurance that the entire family is totally committed, it's not a good idea. However, there are other ways to be involved with this issue; many organizations make it easy for someone with a tender heart to nurture the children in the foster system and support the parents who have chosen to make so many sacrifices to care for them.

We can do better as a society and community. We can offer hope. We can offer home. We can offer forever.

TAKE ACTION

WHAT CAN **ONE** DO?
Open your door

SEVEN YEARS AGO, I met a vibrant young mom who was tutoring the Wellspring Living girls in math. From the first time I met Kara Kiefer, I was so intrigued with her uncanny ability to connect with the girls. The longer Kara worked with the girls and saw their transformation, the more passionate she became. Her heart was tender for their pain. She began to do even more outside tutoring to raise awareness and revenue for our work.

As our friendship continued to develop, I discovered that she and her husband, Russ, had always wanted a third child, but wanted to adopt. A couple of years ago, they began to search for adoption agencies in Atlanta. What they discovered was that this avenue of adoption was expensive and came with mixed results.

Russ and Kara then turned to the option of fostering to adopt through the Division of Families and Children. When this process became stagnant, they felt discouraged. In November of this past year, a friend introduced the Kiefers to Wayne Naugle with Uniting Hope for Children. From the moment they met Wayne, they felt supported, encouraged, and empowered to move forward. They signed up to take the IMPACT training in January and by June, Russ and Kara welcomed a precious little boy. They were encouraged to progress a few steps at a time, so the adoption isn't complete at the time of this writing. However, the experience has proven to be both hard and rewarding. Kara communicated that at the beginning, she felt a roller coaster of emotions. She went on to explain, "If you had asked me a week ago, I probably would've told you that it wasn't going to work out. What we've learned is we have to be 'on our game' all the time. The good news is we are beginning to see a change. We've realized we have to be a hundred percent consistent and overly love him, because his stability is chaos, where our stability is love, order, and consistency. Our hope is this little bundle of 'snips and snails and puppy dogs tails' will sometime soon become our son."

Another door you could open

If becoming a foster parent isn't something you can do, here are other options:

Volunteer to be a mentor for a child at risk.

Locate a local foster care and adoption agency or ministry and help out in one or more of these ways to strengthen a family who is fostering a child:

Provide meals once a month.

Volunteer to help out with transportation.

Write encouraging notes.

Offer to tutor a child.

Become a mentor.

Engage with a foster care agency to inquire about supporting a biological family that is struggling to care for their child(ren).

Provide opportunities to meet "felt" needs as appropriate and directed by the agency.

Provide "technical" assistance to advance the family's stability.

Write encouraging notes to the family.

Share a meal once a month with the family.

WHAT CAN MORE THAN **ONE** DO?
Mentoring circles

Enlist your circle of friends, church, civic group, or company, to work with a local school to create mentoring circles. Once a week or twice a month, host a before-school breakfast or after-school gathering where students meet with trained adults. Make arrangements for food, group activities, and one-on-one encouragement.

Empathy building

Can you imagine leaving the comfort of your family and having to move in with total strangers? This is what happens every day to foster and adopted children across the United States and around the world. Host an experiential event for a group of your friends. When guests walk in the door, they must change into different clothes (supply old clothes in all sizes to choose from); serve strange combinations of food for dinner. Show *Short Term 12* or another movie that expounds on the "real life" of a foster care child.

TEACH **ONE**
Unpredictable

Melissa and Greg had begun their training to become foster parents. They had learned much about the challenges for families. Since becoming a foster family is a commitment for everyone in the family, it was important to Greg and Melissa for their son, Ian, to also understand the challenge, not only for them, but also for the child who might enter their home soon. Take a peek at Melissa's journal:

Melissa's Story:

Sometimes you have to try to walk in someone else's shoes to be able to understand and love them better. As our family explores foster-care-to-adoption, we took on an experiment by changing up our daily routine for twenty-four hours and trying to imagine what it might be like for a potential child coming into our home, where everything they know would suddenly be different and unpredictable.

As a small family of three, we are quite comfortable and go about as we please. Our only son doesn't know what it's like to share on a daily basis with a sibling or to look after one. His daily routine is usually unthreatened by anyone else's preferences or ideas. He plays his own way, watches the TV shows he likes, and gets first pick at the dinner table. So taking on this experiment produced tension fast, especially for him. In twenty-four hours, we ate Lebanese food, discussed other cultures, and had a more defined routine than usual. These simple exercises helped us consider what life would be like for someone entering our home and trying to adjust to a whole new set of norms.

We also watched *Blindside* together and asked our son to imagine being taken away from home and only being able to take two objects with him into another family's home (as is standard with foster children). Then we asked him to really do it for a day. Since he is nine and toys and games are his life, this was when he experienced shock. Ultimately, Ian chose pen and paper for drawing, and Scattergories, one of our family's favorite games.

Giving up favorite foods, freedoms, and things in order to understand what it would be like for someone else to really lose them is quite revealing. For us, the temporary sacrifice led to some soul-searching and good conversations. Even if our adoption journey doesn't pan out, we are glad we experienced a day to sympathize with others and reflect on the conveniences, love, and stability we easily take for granted in our home. Sometimes it's easy to forget.

The social experiment the family tried is below. Will you consider trying it?

Change your family's routine totally for twenty-four hours.

Eat a food from a totally different culture, have a completely different bedtime routine, institute different household expectations (i.e., if you normally don't make your child ask for permission to get something from the fridge, make them ask permission all day long; or make them take their shoes off at the door, etc.).

Be creative to come up with a list of things that might be different in someone else's home.

Have conversations about how it feels to suddenly have everything be different.

Ask these questions: Do you know anyone at your school who is in foster care? How can you help them to feel better and feel more accepted?

A report of child abuse is made
every ten seconds.[1]

The United States has one of the worst
records among industrialized nations—losing
an average between four and seven children
every day to child abuse and neglect.[2]

Individuals who reported six or more
adverse childhood experiences had an
average life expectancy two decades
shorter than those who reported none.[3]

Every year more than 3 million reports of
child abuse are made in the United States
involving more than 6 million children
(a report can include multiple children).[4]

In 2012, state agencies identified an
estimated 1,640 children who died as a
result of abuse and neglect—between
four and five children a day. However,
studies also indicate significant
undercounting of child maltreatment
fatalities by state agencies—by
50 percent or more.[5]

PART FOUR

ZERO
ABUSE

1. A corrupt practice or custom

2. Improper or excessive use or treatment

3. Physical maltreatment[6]

CHAPTER 11

ONE TRAINED, TEN SAFER

Darkness cannot drive out darkness;
only light can do that. Hate cannot drive
out hate; only love can do that.
—DR. MARTIN LUTHER KING JR.

WHEN I FIRST MET THE GIRL in Wellspring Living, I had no idea that what brought her to this place of desperation was having been sold and bought against her will.

I'll never forget the summer evening we sat on the swing in my backyard and she told me about her uncle raping her at the age of five. The reality of what this person, whom she loved and trusted, did to this little girl's body and soul sent a torrent of emotions roiling through me.

This wouldn't be the last time I heard that story or a version of it. The next young woman who walked through our doors had a similar story, as did the next and the next. It became apparent that while the women's stories of destruction (prostitution, being trafficked, drug use) weren't identical, they all had an eerily similar beginning. I became driven to find out more about how this travesty plays out on children.

Do you remember the campaigns in the 1980s and '90s called "Stranger Danger" and "Good Touch/Bad Touch"? These campaigns encouraged parents to teach their children how to identify unsafe people, as if a young, innocent child should—or even could—have that level of discernment. I initially thought those programs, while useful tools to a point, were great; after all, anything that's done to keep our children safe is a step in the right direction, right? But when I realized what we were asking of our children, it was easy to see the limitations of such a campaign. How can a child truly identify an unsafe person, especially when so many of the perpetrators are people they know and are even encouraged to love?

> **The program has made a real difference, particularly as people in positions of influence began to help spread its teachings.**

I'm so grateful for Ann Lee, who personally experienced the violation of childhood sexual abuse, for her work in pinpointing this misconception and creating a better solution. In 1999, she approached Elizabeth Ralston, PhD, executive director of Lowcountry Children's Center in Charleston, South Carolina, about the need for a solution. They joined together to champion the concept that adults, not children, were responsible for preventing child sexual abuse. After all, adults are the ones who are better equipped, both intellectually and emotionally, to work to stop it. Ann formed Darkness to Light under the umbrella of Elizabeth's organization and together they brought this issue to the forefront. It seems so intuitive, yet across generations, children have carried the weight of sexual abuse, often by themselves. In our culture, we tend to believe adults over children, so it is the perfect setup for the abuser.

Working together, these dynamic women forged a pioneering training that revolutionized the approach for the prevention of childhood sexual abuse, initially with the publication of a documentary, television ads, and then the book *7 Steps to Protecting Our Children*. In developing numerous television and radio segments, Darkness to Light knew that a comprehensive training program must be developed. In 2005, the Stewards of Children program was made available for parents, youth-serving organizations, and communities across the nation and globe. In 2006, *Stewards of Children ONLINE* was released as a web-based version of the "live" or facilitated version of the training program. Interested adults can go online, pay a nominal fee, and be armed with a world of knowledge to help protect their own children and children in their communities.

The program has made a real difference, particularly as people in positions of influence began to help spread its teachings. Bridgette Barker, a dynamic and motivated woman who works as the victim's service coordinator for Georgia's Lumpkin County sheriff's office, is a volunteer trainer for Darkness to Light. Because the county had seen a steep increase of sexual abuse cases, Bridgette wanted to do something proactive to see those incidents decrease. She sought funding and began a monthly training using the Darkness to Light curriculum in 2010. Bridgette remembers that first Tuesday evening workshop well.

Bridgette's Story:

I arrived an hour before the training at Lumpkin County Middle School. My team set up drinks and snacks, arranged chairs and tables, and double-checked the audio/video equipment. Then we waited to see if anyone would show up. To my delight, around 7:00 p.m. we began with twenty participants from various walks of life within the community. One major component of our training is showing videos of abuse survivors and identifying telltale behavioral signs that can point to the presence of abuse.

I noticed that one of the attendees seemed to be especially moved throughout the evening, her eyes even welling with tears as she watched the videos and heard the case studies. When I came to the office the next day, I found out that same woman made an incident report at midnight, the night of the training, on an abuse case involving her daughter. She'd watched as her own precious child's behavior and demeanor had changed over the preceding months and recognized the signs—isolation, fear of being around men, sporadic anger, emotional outbursts—that totaled up in her mind. She went home from the training and had a conversation with her daughter, who shared about the ongoing abuse by an extended family member. The woman was devastated, but encouraged that she could get her daughter the help she needed and protect her moving forward. The perpetrator is now serving jail time.

I continue to be astounded about the results that come from this training curriculum. *From that first training until today, I have seen victims identify their abuse and abusers and begin healing; in fact, numerous reports have been made as a direct result of the program.*

In another powerful incident, the local board of education made the training available to education employees, from school nurses and administrators to teachers and bus drivers. Jimmy, a local bus driver, took my course and a few weeks later witnessed something that may well have saved a young girl from being abused. He was driving a middle school girls' soccer team to a tournament outside the state, and he watched as a male coach flirted with and had one of the players sit on his lap during part of the long drive. Alarm signals went off in his mind, and he reported what he'd seen to the school's administrators and to local authorities. The coach was investigated and it quickly became apparent that he had made advances on and even molested four other girls. He was brought to justice and, fortunately, the young soccer player was saved from abuse.

Bridgette continues to train at the local college and has found the funding to offer all interested educators/school employees in her county access to the training free of charge. In addition, she trains physical therapists, nurses, criminal justice staff, and the community at large. Anyone who is interested in learning what to look for to prevent childhood abuse can take the two-and-a-half-hour training classes. Bridgette says that every time she trains a group she has one or two victims come forward or reports made that are the direct results from the awareness shared. The success with these trainees drives Bridgette to keep volunteering her time to train in her community. In fact, Darkness to Light shares an astounding statistic about the effect of their training: For every one adult who is trained, ten children are safer.[7]

While programs are effective for awareness and prevention, many times those in the training receive just what they need to move forward in their lives. Sylvia Goalen, a survivor, came to a Stewards of Children training in the Atlanta area and, as a result, became aware of the implications of the sexual abuse she suffered as a child.

Sylvia lived in Guatemala with her six siblings and Mom and Dad. In the Latin American community, families often live together in clusters in order to support each other. Since Sylvia's dad traveled back and forth to the United States to provide for the family, it made sense for her mom and family to rely on the support of their family nearby. Unfortunately, this arrangement led to Sylvia becoming prey for a family member. Sylvia explained how the situation played out:

Sylvia's Story:

When my mom would go out with the other moms to go shopping, she would leave me with my older cousins. My sixteen-year-old cousin targeted me. He was charismatic and everyone liked him. He was a natural leader. He stole my innocence, and I was never the same. I felt like I had no control and that no one would believe me anyway.

Years later, when our family was planning on moving to be with my father in the United States, my mother told me that a family member was going to move with us because he needed to raise some money and get his life together. At sixteen, I remember coming home from high school one afternoon to discover that this family member was that same cousin who had raped me as a child. I told my mom and dad what had happened, and they insisted that I deal with this on my own and left it to me to confront him.

I gathered up my courage and did speak to him, but when my parents were out of earshot, he threatened me. He pinned me against the wall and he said to me, "If you keep going on about this, I'm going to show you what I should have showed you years ago. That will really teach you a lesson." I came to find out that the same kinds of abuse happened to some of my cousins and other family members as well. That happened long ago. I'd been married ten years and had never talked about what happened to me, even with my husband, until I attended a Darkness to Light training.

My husband and I were in the process of adopting a teenage boy, and one of the requirements was to attend this training. As the trainer, Tiffany Sawyer, spoke and shared the video stories, I realized the secret that I had been holding inside was actually affecting my entire life. After the training, I approached Tiffany, who encouraged me to seek out counseling. A lot of things came together after that training. My husband and I were able to understand why certain things triggered me, and I began to finally heal from a trauma I had experienced over twenty years earlier. It's been a tremendous gift to get to be honest about what's happened to me and to live out from under the weight of carrying a secret.

Today, Sylvia works for the fire department and is a trainer for Darkness to Light. She especially volunteers to train in the Hispanic community. Sylvia thinks of other little girls—boys too—who could be at risk from predators and wants to bring awareness and prevention.

Darkness to Light now has more than 7,700 authorized facilitators who teach the program in fifty states and seventeen international locations, and more than 920,000 copies of the training have been distributed to communities around the world.

CHAPTER 12

ONE WAY TO
SAVE A LIFE

Wherever the art of medicine is loved,
there is also a love of humanity.
—HIPPOCRATES

BEFORE MY WORK with Wellspring Living, I had no idea the extent of medical issues that could result from childhood trauma. For the first time in my life, I met young women who had survived horrific life circumstances with multiple residual effects of their pain.

It was shocking to me the number of medical visits needed with each woman. From stomach issues to skin irritations, fainting spells to migraine headaches and aches and pains galore, it seemed like every day there were more physical complaints. I couldn't reconcile it, since we were providing such a comforting environment for them, certainly better than their most recent experiences. They were eating better, exercising, and engaging in counseling, yet there were ongoing health issues. When I finally came across the Adverse Childhood Experiences Study (ACEs), these chronic symptoms began to make sense.

Dr. Vince Felitti of Kaiser Permanente and Dr. Bob Anda from the Centers for Disease Control and Prevention (CDC) conducted this study, which revealed the connection of adverse childhood experiences (ACEs) with health and social problems in adults. The screening tool assesses the level of trauma experienced, and the results are astounding. Did you know the higher the ACE score, the greater the propensity one has for chronic pulmonary disease, hepatitis, depression, suicidality, lung cancer, and heart disease? Dr. Robert Block, former president of the American Academy of Pediatrics, stated, "Adverse childhood experiences are the single greatest unaddressed public health threat facing our nation today."[8]

One person who is making huge strides to combat this very real risk is Dr. Jordan Greenbaum, medical director of the Stephanie V. Blank Center for Safe and Healthy Children at Children's Healthcare of Atlanta. Her diminutive stature belies her iron will to tackle the issues of sexual abuse and exploitation head-on through educating healthcare professionals.

While she's quick to point out that she's not a pediatrician, as a trained forensic pathologist, she became interested in childhood injury and eventually found her way to studying and preventing child abuse. She spent fifteen years working in children's hospitals, observing and interacting with suspected victims of physical abuse, sexual abuse and neglect. In 2008, she started learning about commercial sexual exploitation of children, which is the worst form of sexual abuse, and she was forever changed. We met in 2009, while working on the statewide task force on trafficking. It became her personal mission to create easily accessible training for medical personnel to assist in victim identification.

As we talked about the complexities of identifying victims, I saw Jordan look toward the floor and spoke in a saddened voice about how she realized that she herself had seen children and teens in the ER and at clinics who displayed the very signs that should have identified them as commercially exploited youth. As she reflected on all the times she'd come face-to-face with a victim without realizing it and had heard others discuss patients with similar symptoms, she realized the very real need for a systematic approach to training the medical world and first responders to be hyperaware to help these victims.

I want you to read this shocking fact aloud: A 2014 study in the *Annals of Health Law* found that 88 percent of victims who had been rescued from sex trafficking said they had seen a physician or medical professional *while* they were being exploited.[9] Now reread that sentence, and let the reality sink in. These girls and boys (yes, boys can be exploited too and it happens more than you might

> **Eighty-eight percent of victims who had been rescued from sex trafficking said they had seen a physician or medical professional *while* they were being exploited.**

think) went to a hospital, doctor's office, or clinic for treatment and were so under the control of their abuser that they didn't disclose the fact that they were being hurt in some of the worst ways imaginable. They were that close to deliverance from their trafficker.

By law in all fifty states, a medical professional has to report abuse of any kind to the local authorities, so the victims didn't get the help they desperately needed. How could they have? They were terrified, and the medical staff they saw likely dismissed them as "bad" kids who had gotten into trouble of their own making.

Jordan now speaks with authority on this issue, approaching the subject with reason. She is methodical, analytical, and appears almost impassive, even her short, straight silver-grey hair a study in efficiency. While she cares deeply for all victims, she's realized that she can make the biggest impact by creating training programs and processes to standardize screening and care. I'd love for you to hear Jordan's point of view and wisdom:

Jordan's Story:

It's easy to think that trafficking only happens in other, less developed countries or, if it happens in the United States at all, that it's far away from "us" and where "our" kids go to school, somewhere out of sight. Let me be the first to tell you: you are *mistaken*.

Take for instance the case of fourteen-year-old Marlee, who, as a solid B student, is doing pretty well in school. She lives at home with her mom after her dad left. Her mom works a lot to make ends meet. She struggles with feelings of abandonment, but soldiers through. Hey, after all, lots of her friends at school were growing up in single-parent homes too. She is just normal.

Like teens tend to do, she sometimes fought with her mom about boundaries and spends a lot of time on Facebook blowing off steam. There she meets a guy, who tells her that he's "a little older." He tells her how beautiful and wonderful she is and asks how her mom can't see all of that about her. As he gains her trust, he fulfills her need for a boyfriend, a father, and a protector, all rolled into one. He tells her he's dying to meet her in person and convinces Marlee to run away while her mom's at work.

He drives her to another city one state over and seals the deal by having sex with her over a few days in a motel. He tells her they're going to build a life together, but first they need some cash. He says, "If you'll just have sex with a couple of other guys, we can get the money we need." Of course, she doesn't want to, but since she thinks she's deeply in love with him, she does it.

He starts feeding her cocktails of drugs to keep her dependent and beats her up to keep her compliant. This horror goes on for seven months. One day, a buyer beats her up so badly that she's hanging on to life by a thread. They decide she's not worth the trouble and anonymously drop her off at the closest emergency room, where she's treated for her injuries. The medical professionals caring for her quickly realize that she's little more than a child and after a bit of research find her in the National Database for Missing and Exploited Children. They transition her into a safe house where she receives counseling and therapy, until eventually she's able to move back home with her mom, who has never stopped looking for her.

Or consider sixteen-year-old Carter. He's been acting out at home and finally his parents kick him out, saying they can't handle his outbursts any longer. He crashes on a friend's couch for a few days, but he quickly runs out of money, so he's officially out on the streets. He's approached by a couple of other homeless boys who say, "You can hang out with us. We take care of each other." They tell him that he has to find a way to make some money, though, and offer to show him how to turn his first trick.

He feels accepted by these kids; it's the kind of easy acceptance he's never gotten anywhere else, so he figures, "Why not? What have I got to lose?" He doesn't like the thought of it, but his "friends" have convinced him that he's actually the one pulling one over on the buyers, turning the tables and taking advantage of them.

Most of us don't realize that males can be victims as well.

After a few months, he gets picked up by law enforcement and treated like an offender, thrown into jail as a prostitute. Upon examination, a jail doc discovers that he has gonorrhea and chlamydia. When he discloses his situation to a counselor, he gets put in a foster home. After all, he's still a minor. However, he doesn't feel accepted by his foster family either and runs away, back to the streets, where his "Band of Brothers" welcomes him. The next time he's picked up, he's again treated as an offender rather than a minor victim, and by the time he's able to get help, he's no longer a minor, and those in a position to help dismiss him as someone who made poor choices.

I hope that these stories—composites of actual youth I've met, as confidentiality prevents me from sharing their real names and exact details—will awaken you to the fact that this *is* happening out in the open. Most people are under the mistaken impression that kids who are exploited commercially are hidden away, without interaction. That's just not true. Instead, if you're a parent, these kids could be in your kid's class at school, since many exploited school-age children and teens are still enrolled in school.

In addition, as you can see from these stories, it's not always a male trafficker and female victim. While that's often what we expect to see, most of us don't realize that males can be victims as well, since culture doesn't objectify boys in the same way as it does girls. In fact, there is a large population of exploited boys, but the medical community, in the past, has tended not to screen them for abuse. While some of them may identify as homosexual, many are not, but may engage in survival sex as a last resort.

In addition, while some youth, as in the case of "Marlee," have parents who are actively looking for them, other kids like "Carter" have been thrown away. No one was looking for him. He was virtually invisible. I've seen more kids than I can count who are vulnerable by virtue of having a drug-addicted parent or one who's never around. Of course, when home life gets so bad and a child runs away, he or she is ripe for exploitation. Kids for whom no one's looking make the perfect victims.

That's where medical professionals' training comes into the equation. Young people may present with depression and an STD, but upon further examination and observation, a savvy school nurse may discover that the teen boy is engaging in survival sex after being kicked out of his home. Or a gynecologist may notice signs of abuse beyond a girl's pregnancy and depression. They just need to know which signs bear further inquiry.

Medical workers and first responders should look for chronic pain without organic cause (like back pain without an injury), changes in behavior, weight loss or changes in appetite, PTSD and nightmares, insomnia, depression or self-harm, genital infections, drug and alcohol use (self-medicating), anxiety or panic, unexplained fatigue or exhaustion. These symptoms only scratch the surface. I should note that, though these things are important for healthcare workers to monitor, they're just as important for parents and anyone who comes in contact with a child to notice as well. Sadly, some parents have no idea what their kids are up to, whether they're doing it on their own or being forced.

Posttraumatic stress disorder is another big one, as 75 percent of kids who have been exploited exhibit these symptoms.[10] Forty percent of exploited youth have tried to commit suicide.[11] This kind of deep-seated trauma isn't cured with a few therapy sessions, particularly since often there hasn't been just one traumatic event. It could have been a pattern over their lifetime. This kind of systematic sexual trauma strips these young people of dignity and self-worth. Toxic stress may affect brain development and can

---

People always ask, "Why wouldn't they ask for help?"

---

damage the rational, analytical part of the brain that can weigh pros and cons, that is, reasonably make decisions. They become wired for certain outbursts or reactions to stress triggers, even small ones.

People always ask, "Why wouldn't they ask for help?" After all, they are alone in an exam room with their doctor or nurse in a seemingly safe place. But they've likely been told not to disclose anything about their "setup" or to lie when asked pressing questions. They may have been threatened within an inch of their lives or been so brainwashed that they see their trafficker as their "boyfriend" and are protecting him. They could be scared that they'd be blamed for everything that's happened and get into more trouble with authorities. Worst of all, they may have become convinced that they're not the victims at all, that really they're the ones exploiting the buyers. When their still-developing young brains and bodies are subjected to this kind of pervasive trauma, it teaches them not to hope, not to share, and not to trust anyone.

For the general public—anyone who cares about a teen or child—here are some important things to consider.

1. Not all kids have an obvious range of risk factors (history of sex abuse, drug abuse, etc.) and yet can still be at risk (particularly from online predators).

2. There is some level of risk for *all* kids, due to their adolescent brains, which are impulsive and not fully able to weigh consequences or see danger.

3. Be aware that anyone could be vulnerable (boys and girls).

4. When kids reach the age to be on the Internet without constant supervision, teach basic online safety such as not disclosing personal information such as name, age, location, and so on. Technology changes quickly, and to many of us, it can seem hard to keep up. However, commonsense use of any social media or other online experience is an essential tool for children and teens to learn and to understand why it is important to be cautious.

5. Be on the lookout for behavioral changes (sleep changes, your child suddenly showing up with expensive items, etc.). Ask questions.

As physicians, we are adept at treating symptoms. When a bone is broken, we set it. When a disease crops up, we treat it. But peeling back the layers to see the heart of the issue, especially one as complex as exploitation and abuse, is much more complicated.

I've worked to create training curriculum for medical professionals and anyone who works with children, as well as first responders. As part of this, we have a six-part webinar series and online modules, all of which are free. In addition, we have a simple six-question screening tool in the works, which we are hoping to validate soon.

Finally, we are encouraging use of child advocacy centers and community protocols, which minimize the number of times the survivor must tell his or her story, and optimize access to resources for treatment to get everything needed to begin treatment, rather than having to tell the story of abuse over and over to a police officer or detective first, then doctor, then social worker, etc.

As a country, we have to take a macro approach to this issue. Having human trafficking in a democracy undermines and erodes our freedom and goes against the very foundation of our free nation. Modern slavery is real. We talk about how far we've come, but it's going on under our noses, impacting our next generation of adults. The cost of treating kids who become adults, paying for mental and physical healthcare, lost income, and incarceration are prices we cannot afford. Everyone pays, and everyone suffers, either directly or indirectly. We have to safeguard every child in America to truly be free.

Because of Dr. Jordan Greenbaum's diligent work, I know one of our survivors was able to receive services. Katie had been in the clutches of a trafficking ring that was operating inside an upscale hotel in Atlanta, no one the wiser. Law enforcement seemed to be closing in on the ring, and the trafficker moved Katie to an extended-stay hotel in a neighboring county. As the pressure of law enforcement increased, the temper of her trafficker escalated, and Katie felt she would be killed in his next violent outburst. So when he was out, Katie was able to make a 911 call and was taken to the emergency room of a local hospital. The nurse on duty had just completed Child Sex Trafficking in America training and made a call to get Katie into the services she needed. Today, Katie will tell you that if it hadn't been for that savvy ER nurse, she would most likely be dead. One life saved is always worth it.

TAKE ACTION

WHAT CAN **ONE** DO?

Sign up today to take the Darkness to Light Training (http://www.d2l.org/site /c.4dICIJOkGcISE/b.6143709/k.3D5F/Child_Sexual _Abuse_Prevention_Training_ONLINE.htm)

Affirmation

DO ALL YOU CAN to keep children in your circle of influence affirmed. Initiate conversations that recognize their unique value through conversations of affirmation. Children most often will respond to your suggestions and feel comfortable letting you know if someone isn't acting appropriately toward them. Here are some phrases of affirmation:

You're thoughtful

You're a good listener

You're helpful

You have great ideas

You're a good friend

You're brave

You have a great sense of humor

You are a hard worker

You work well with others

You are diligent

You are responsible

You are creative

Investigate questionable behaviors, no matter who it is. Over 80 percent of all child abuse cases reported occur with people who are familiar with the child (family or friends).[12] Report any incident to the police. Often, it isn't the first time the perpetrator has abused someone.

WHAT CAN MORE THAN **ONE** DO?
Celebrate

Host a party celebrating and affirming children in your community. Invite friends and family over for a celebration with the children in their lives. Every adult is asked to bring a child(ren) in their family or one they mentor and make one comment for each that expresses something uniquely positive about the child they support. Create a special way each child will be celebrated. Create a wall hanging or a scrapbook with these comments and pictures of the celebration as a keepsake. At the end of the evening, adults can share proclamations similar to this:

Tonight, we proclaim that _____ is someone I (we) believe has potential for greatness. Because of this, I (we) want you to grow up in a way that reflects your best self. I (We) want everyone to appreciate your unique qualities and honor your life. We commit to always believe in you and help you grow up in safety and love. (If this celebration is part of a church or other faith-based event, you might add something like, "We want you to grow up to be the person God created you to be.")

Training for all

Engage your circles to help raise funds so that teachers, bus drivers, school janitors, cafeteria workers, other caretakers of children, etc., are trained in your community.

TEACH **ONE**
Equip your child

Make sure your child understands that he or she can share anything with you, even if it's hard to hear, and you will always believe in them. It is the responsibility of adults to keep children safe. At the same time, we must equip our children with facts about appropriate touch and give permission for them to say no when they are uncomfortable. It is vital that children feel heard and safe telling responsible adults when something uncomfortable is occurring. The timing of these conversations could take place at bath time or bedtime or before beginning a new venture (school, summer camp, day care, etc.).

One method of conversation is to play the "what-if" game with your child.

Suggest scenarios like these to give your child practice saying no.

You are walking home from the playground or a friend's home and someone you don't know comes up and offers a ride. What do you say?

Someone comes by in a car and says your mother asked him to pick you up and take you home. What do you do? What do you say? Who do you tell?

Someone touches your body in a place that is covered by a swimsuit. What do you say? Who do you tell?

Someone you don't know says they will give you a piece of candy if you come with them. What do you say? Who do you tell? Or someone you don't know asks you to come and help him find his lost dog. What do you say? Who do you tell?

Teach your children that adults should ask other adults for help, not kids.

Create a follow-up plan of action.

70 percent of all sex trafficking victims were former foster children. [1]

More than 100,000 children are currently trafficked for sex in the United States. [2]

In 2014, the National Human Trafficking Resource Center Hotline received reports of 3,598 sex trafficking cases inside the United States. [3]

The average age of a child when they first are used in prostitution is twelve to fourteen years old. [4]

PART FIVE

ZERO TRAFFICKING

"The recruitment, harboring, transportation, provision, or obtaining of a person for the purpose of a commercial sex act where such an act is induced by force, fraud, or coercion."[5]

CHAPTER 13

ONE GOOD FIT

Unless someone like you cares a whole awful lot,
nothing is going to get better. It's not.
—*THE LORAX* BY DR. SEUSS

ON A SPRING MORNING in April, Jada was born, seven pounds, eight ounces of sheer innocence and beauty. Her mom, Bernice, was only nineteen, and Jada's dad was nowhere to be found. The day she came home from the hospital, Bernice put a pair of crocheted pink shoes on Jada's tiny baby feet and resolved to do the best she knew how for her daughter.

As Jada grew into a little girl, it was clear that she faced difficult odds. She loved her mom dearly and wanted to be just like her, somewhat heartbreaking in itself, since Bernice was in and out of prison and addicted to a combination of hard-core drugs, any one of which could derail anyone's life.

Like many little girls, one of Jada's favorite childhood games was to play dress up, trying on Bernice's too-big clothes and putting on her makeup. Dresses, sweaters, blush, and eye shadow became some of her favorite toys. With sweet childlike innocence, Jada would go into her mom's closet, trying on her shoes and pretending to "walk like Mommy." These oversized high-heeled shoes told a story of the world Jada lived in, one where she didn't seem to fit or have a place.

Bernice had problems of her own, so she struggled to reciprocate Jada's love and failed to provide for even the child's most basic needs, to say nothing of the emotional nurturing a young girl craves. She couldn't seem to hold down a job, and Jada was passed from her grandmother to her aunties most of her young life.

One afternoon walking home from school, a group of older boys took advantage of this precious second grader. Jada was left with one more scar on her little life, physical ones, yes, but the emotional scars ran even deeper. With no adult in her life to advocate for and take responsibility for her health and safety, Jada began to wear the most unattractive and ill-fitting clothes and shoes she could find, so maybe, no one would notice her or bother her ever again.

> **Jada would do anything for Julius. She referred lovingly to him as "Daddy."**

Life continued to be full of chaos and uncertainty. Jada's grandmother was stretched to her limit caring for not only Jada but other grandchildren as well. So, when Jada turned thirteen, she put on her hand-me-down running shoes and, unnoticed, easily ran away from home. *Surely, I'll be better on my own*, she thought. At first she stayed with the families of friends she knew from school, but none of these places lasted more than a few weeks. It became harder and harder to go to school and keep up with her work.

Within two short months, Jada's running shoes led her to a place of hunger and homelessness. That's when she met Julius, twenty-nine, outside a local fast-food restaurant. Julius offered to buy her a meal and listened as she told him tidbits of her story. He gave her just enough attention to convince her that he would rescue her and love her like no other person had in her life thus far.

He invited her home with him, offering her a roof over her head and the kind of security she craved so desperately. Jada would do anything for Julius. She now referred lovingly to him as "Daddy." After all, he bought her sexy clothes and stiletto shoes and made her feel beautiful. For the first three weeks, Jada had never felt so much love. She was convinced her life would finally be on a better path. This short-lived joy ended abruptly when "Daddy" brought three other friends over one evening. It was a night full of violence and sex that left scar after scar on her young body and her tender heart. Even though Jada was forced to live with five other girls and offer her services up to ten times a night, she was still sure that Julius loved her.

A neighbor at the normal-looking apartment complex in the suburbs became suspicious of the cast of characters coming and going at all times of the day and night and called local authorities. Through an FBI sting, Jada was rescued, along with the other girls held captive. But Jada didn't believe she needed to be rescued. She kept saying to the officers, "I need to get back to Daddy. He will be so worried about me."

The first time I saw Jada was when she walked onto the Wellspring Living campus in Atlanta with her towering black six-inch stiletto heels. Her ankles were wobbly as she tried to navigate the three steps leading into the home. The now fifteen-year-old was trying hard to match what Julius had expected of her over the past eleven months. Despite the fact that "Daddy" wasn't there, Jada held on to her stiletto shoes as if it was a part of her identity. "After all, Daddy wants me to always wear these shoes. They make me look more attractive to him," she would explain when we asked if she wanted to get more comfortable shoes from the clothes closet.

For the first few weeks, Jada didn't even consider that she could make any decisions other than the ones "Daddy" had trained her to make.

One day Christina, the coach Jada chose, asked her, "Did you *want* to do everything 'Daddy' asked you to do?"

"No . . . but I have to please him," she replied.

Christina kept presenting to Jada the idea that she should have choices based on her own needs and her own dreams. Day after day, consistent love, care, respect and the opportunity to make choices began to have an effect on Jada's thinking. Over time, we saw change occur. The first indication that Jada was considering advocating for herself was the day she said, "Miss Christina, could you take me to the clothes closet? I want to get a pair of shoes that actually fit me." So down we went, into our beautiful closet, with rows of new shoes. She thoughtfully walked along the rows, running her slim fingers along athletic shoes in her favorite colors, each tied with pristine laces. Her eyes lit up as she pointed to a pair, brightly colored in neon pink and royal purple and just her size. "These are the ones!" she told us.

We watched with delight as Jada continued to grow into her true self, with a bounce in her step. She took those shoes to our sports courts, running and playing volleyball and basketball. Her contagious smile began to make regular appearances, as she grew comfortable being who God had created her to be. She came to know she was empowered to make choices in her life and have people that would support her in ways that continue to make her better.

After ten months in the program, it was time for Jada to graduate and be adopted into a local family that would love her and foster her dreams. That day was all about Jada, filled with love and affirmation. In her brief speech to the other girls in the program, staff, and volunteers, she said, "My journey's been hard. There were lots of times I wanted to quit, lots of times I thought I couldn't go on. I couldn't have done it without Miss Christina. She helped me when I thought I couldn't put one foot in front of the other. So to all of you, just keep walking forward. It's so worth it!"

Jada moves confidently now, filled with the kind of hope, pride, dignity and self-esteem that only come from knowing who you are. And of course, on her feet, you'll find shoes that she picked out—ones that fit.

REACT

What are some things in Jada's life that didn't fit? Later, what are some things that did fit? Can you relate to things in your own life that fit and didn't fit? Do you know a child who needs a "good fit" in some way?

CHAPTER 14

THE POWER
OF ONE

*The willingness to share does not make one
charitable, it makes one free.*
—ROBERT BRAULT

I MET DAVE MCCLEARY in the halls of the Passion conference, a convention of more than twenty thousand college students, in January 2012. Wellspring Living was honored to be a part of the conference, during which one of our graduates, Melissa, had the opportunity to tell her riveting—and to those who aren't aware, incredible story on CNN. I was in the room at Philips Arena, next door to the meganews network in Atlanta with her and the film crew while she was interviewed.

Later that day, after the video was broadcast, both on the CNN network and on the big screens at Passion, there was a palpable sense of awe over the entire building. As I walked into the hallway, I almost ran headlong into this man, sort of shaking his head and trying to get control of his emotions. Tears welling up in his eyes he was physically touched by what he'd just seen on the screen. In his soft-spoken voice, this distinguished middle-aged man introduced himself as Dave McCleary. He said, "I have to do something with what I just heard. I just don't know what yet."

I went on to learn that he was a successful business owner, based in an affluent suburb of Atlanta and, before that day, he believed that the issue of human trafficking couldn't play a real role in his own community. He was about to find out how incorrect that assumption was.

Dave's history may sound like a lot of people's—going through life, working to earn a living and raise a family. But he also exemplifies the extraordinary qualities of someone willing to sacrifice for a purpose. He felt the tug on his heartstrings to make an impact with however much or little influence he has, and it's taken the movement against human trafficking forward in a big way. So, I think he's the best one to tell you his own story.

Dave's Story:

I've lived my whole life in Fulton County, Georgia, the largest county cutting across metro Atlanta. With hard work, I've built a thriving business with forty employees, cleaning and maintaining large schools and churches in the area. My wife, two daughters, and I lived in a clean-cut, middle-class suburb, happily thinking that our experience with our own city was typical.

I decided to volunteer for the Passion conference for the first time in 2012. Most first-time male volunteers get assigned to direct parking outside the massive Philips Arena complex, removed from the action. However, I was pleased that my assignment was to serve as a door greeter inside the auditorium, so I would hear every speaker over the course of the three-day event. Looking back now, I know that wasn't an accident.

It was powerful to see so many motivated college students gathered together, rallying around the big issues in our world—lack of clean drinking water, poverty, homelessness, education, and yes, slavery. As a Christian conference, it's designed to motivate tangible action for the attendees, with a goal of changing the world for the better. I was surprised that one of the main focuses was human trafficking, and not just internationally, but right here in the United States (in Atlanta, even). My first thought was, *Why in the world would they be talking about such a heavy issue? Surely that's not a sizeable enough problem here at home that it warrants the focus of a conference for college students.* I was about to discover how wrong I was.

As I listened to the stories of abuse, violence, and slavery that were going on domestically, one in particular caught my attention. During Passion, CNN did a story on Melissa. While the woman on the screen could have been anyone you'd see next to you pumping gas or shopping at your neighborhood grocery, as she told her story, a much darker chain of events unfolded.

As a sixteen-year-old runaway, Melissa spent a year and a half being bought and sold against her will, all virtually in my backyard. After an anonymous stranger helped her escape her captor, in 2001 she eventually found her way to the newly minted Wellspring Living program and went on to become its first graduate.

The usually noisy group was silent, sitting in rapt attention as this diminutive brunette started to tell her story.

Needless to say, I was shocked. Following the conference, I reached out to Mary Frances, because I wanted to have Melissa, now a well-adjusted mother and wife, come speak to my Roswell chapter of the Rotary Club, an organization of community leaders, businesspeople, educators, and politicians. You see, I was nearing the end of my term as the president of my chapter of nearly 350 members, and I wanted to capitalize on the opportunity to educate them on the real dangers facing our community and maybe, just maybe, motivate us as a group to take some kind of action. Needless to say, my fellow board members were surprised that I wanted to present such a grave issue at one of our meetings. *Just wait*, I thought.

The day Melissa came to the Roswell Rotary Club to speak on a panel, the gym where we meet was packed, filled with nearly three hundred members. The usually noisy group was silent, sitting in rapt attention as this diminutive brunette started to tell her story. "I grew up in a home that was very lonely, chaotic, and confusing," she began. "I ran away from home at seventeen because I was desperate and was in and out of horrible, abusive relationships. In fact, I was raped multiple times by the time I was seventeen."

Melissa went on to share about how she and a roommate rented a respectable-looking town house and had low-wage jobs. When a neighbor came by to borrow their phone, he asked her if she'd ever considered modeling or working as an escort. She told him that she didn't need a job at the time, but tucked his business card away. Soon though, she found herself unemployed and called him. The "easy" work that seemed too good to be true, in fact, was. Quickly, the man moved into her apartment, feeding her a steady diet of drugs—and not much else—controlling everything she did and everyone she saw.

At nineteen she was rushed to the hospital for an overdose so serious that her heart was in danger of exploding. After doctors helped her detox and released her from their care, she was terrified; but plagued by the Stockholm Syndrome (developing empathy for a captor or abuser), she was intent on returning to her pimp. In a twist of fate, she was arrested for an outstanding traffic ticket on her way back to the town house. Police helped her enter the Wellspring Living program, where she spent intense time inching toward the healing that would allow her to lead a full, productive life.

You could have heard a pin drop when she finished speaking, the audience was so captivated by her strength, vulnerability, and recovery.

After the panel, I stood at the front, watching some of our Rotarians come up to speak with Melissa. One member in particular, threw one arm around her and gave her a quick hug. As Melissa walked away, I approached my friend and asked how he knew her. "She used to babysit my children when she was a student at the local high school," he replied. "I haven't seen her in years."

I was stunned. My two daughters went to that very same high school. From that moment forward, I couldn't look at this issue as something distant or that didn't affect me. Suddenly, it had my own precious children's faces on it, and I knew that I had to do whatever I could and leverage whatever resources I had at my disposal to make a difference. I didn't know what, exactly, we were going to do, but I knew we had to do something.

After hearing such a powerful story, my Rotary chapter was intent on engaging in the community to end human trafficking, but that didn't seem enough. So I called some fellow Rotarians from other metro Atlanta chapters and began speaking at their meetings. Again, it didn't seem like enough. I branched out and traveled around the state, sharing this unbelievable story to any clubs that would have me. Through Melissa's story and my own, I was able to help put a loved one's face on this issue, making

it real to people who may have never considered
the very real threat to our young people. As a result,
I was invited to join the Georgia governor's Task
Force for Human Trafficking.

Then, the "Rotary Zone," the twenty-nine
districts that span from Virginia to the Caribbean,

**I always ask myself, "What
is one life worth?" and the
only answer I can come back
with is "Everything."**

---

had their annual meeting of six hundred leaders,
and I was asked to sit on a panel. That got the other
leaders fired up and all the clubs along the eastern
seaboard began talking about this vital issue at their
own meetings. Now it's spreading on across the
United States, and we've created an action group
called "Rotarians Against Child Slavery." The goal
is to make it an international cause and to engage the
more than 1.2 million Rotary members around the
world to eradicate this issue permanently, much like
the organization's involvement spurred the availabil-
ity of polio vaccinations worldwide. Polio is largely
stamped out now, and I believe that we can be instrumental in similarly stamping out human trafficking.

What I've learned during this journey is that any
child—boy or girl, rich or poor—can be at risk of

being taken advantage of. There have been times when getting this message out has been tough, requiring sacrifices not only of me, but of my family and my business. But I always ask myself, "What is one life worth?" and the only answer I can come back with is "Everything."

I've had people say that what I've done is "amazing" or "incredible," but I always feel like I was so clearly presented with this opportunity and the only thing I could do was walk forward.

One person can't do everything, but I encourage anyone who is touched by this issue—whether they see their child's face on it, or their grandchild's face or the face of a child they don't even know—to pick one thing in their own sphere of influence and do that thing. You never know where it will take you or whose life you'll save.

Over the years I've talked to many people who are touched by this issue. It stirs their hearts on an emotional level, but few follow through with what they think they can do. Dave isn't that kind of person. He not only took the first step to begin to bring support around the issue, but he kept walking down the road of advocacy and engagement. The road wasn't easy; it's been filled with lots of obstacles and difficult conversations, but he's stayed true to the course. So much has been accomplished through Rotary in the intervening years since 2012. If it weren't for the determination and the power behind this one man, Dave McCleary, none of it would have been achieved.

TAKE ACTION

WHAT CAN **ONE** DO?

IMAGINE HOW IT MUST FEEL to not have shoes that fit and the obstacles you would face if you had to wear shoes that didn't fit every day. Now imagine if you never felt like you fit into life like everyone else. Seek to understand what it must feel like when a vulnerable boy or girl feels like he or she might never fit in. Discuss with some friends and journal your thoughts.

Are you ready to be the ONE who makes a difference for ONE child? You could provide a pair of shoes for a child you know needs one. You could also connect with the amazing organization Shoes That Fit.

Shoes That Fit is a national organization that has given out more than a million pairs of new shoes (and new items of clothing), working with local schools to meet the practical clothing and footwear needs of students. Like us, and like Jada, they know that new shoes help offer dignity, hope, pride, and self-esteem to children. It matters! Visit www.shoesthatfit.org, find one of the many local chapters across the country, and purchase shoes to donate. Or start your own chapter in your own city or town.

Be ONE who makes a difference! Here are some ideas:

Journal about how much shoes that fit—or don't—can affect how you feel about yourself.

Find a child you know who has a need for new shoes and

provide them. Don't make a big deal about it—being in need can feel shameful and this experience should be all about encouraging that kid. Tell them how important they are and all of the great places they'll go in their shiny new shoes.

Donate anonymously to a kid who needs a new pair of shoes through Shoes That Fit (www.shoesthatfit.org).

WHAT CAN MORE THAN **ONE** DO?
A special closet

One summer, my good friend Jenn Benecke asked to meet me for coffee. At the time, she worked as the president of the Junior League of Atlanta, a group of more than 3,500 members who are committed to serving the community. Jenn was looking for a creative project her team could do to impact our work at Wellspring Living, with girls who are survivors of trafficking. Atlanta is one of the largest trafficking hubs in the United States and this group of passionate, service-minded women wanted to make a difference.

After brainstorming, we came up with the idea that the Junior League of Atlanta would create a clothes closet filled with stylish clothes, shoes, and toiletries so each girl who enters our program could go in and pick out everything she needed. It was important to us that the items be new, never used, and the right sizes, so girls would know that they're not a second thought or second class in any way. They matter, and for some of them, it would be the first time in their life they'd been valued enough to have brand-new things.

This action-oriented group of women made it fun for their members, engaging them to make a real difference.

The women made it fun, going in groups to purchase items from our wish list, including clothing and shoes in every size needed for teenage girls. The result was vanloads of beautiful, functional clothes our girls are proud to wear. What a special way to show dignity and love to the girls! Now when a girl enters the Wellspring Living home, she can go to the clothes closet and pick out an outfit and shoes she likes and that fit her.

Shoes for everyone

Are you ready to make a difference in your own community, perhaps for children and teens you've never met? Here are some ideas:

Locate an elementary or middle school or nonprofit that works with underserved children.

Ask if you can make shoes anonymously available.

Gather shoe sizes.

Galvanize a team to purchase shoes for each child.

In each shoebox, write a personal note of encouragement.

Deliver them anonymously.

TEACH **ONE**
Build compassion

My husband, Dick, and I love keeping our grandsons. We always have so much fun together! Art and science projects, golf cart rides, hiking, and playing at the park are some of our favorites. That's what grandparents are for, right? Recently, I watched Cal,

Rett, and Sam come running down our driveway, ready for a fun afternoon with us. As I observed them running around, expending a surplus of energy, as only little boys can do, the thought crossed my mind: they have always had shoes that fit.

I've been told often that the time and lessons grandparents share with their grandchildren potentially make deeper impressions than even their parents. With this thought in mind, I wanted to create a teachable moment with them. I looked through our closet and found several pairs of oversized shoes. My husband wears size 13 shoes, so Cal, our eight-year-old, instinctively chose those, and Rett, our five-year-old, chose the ones that were big for him, a size 9.

I challenged the boys to see what happened when they tried to walk around their house, run outside, play basketball, etc. As they were participating in the activities, Cal and Rett told me how they felt. Cal said, "It's not easy to do anything in these shoes. They are so heavy!" Rett, who kept walking out of his shoes, looked at me and said, "I thought it would be fun, but this is hard." Obviously, it was impossible to maintain their level of high energy with these shoes that didn't fit.

After our activities, I began to ask questions like, "Do you know someone who has shoes that don't fit?" and "How do you think they feel?" Our conversations turned to questions like, "Do you know someone who always feels left out or doesn't fit into your class or team?" I love the thoughtfulness that emerged. Cal said to me, "Mimi, I think it is important to be a friend to people who feel left out. I had this boy in my class who was very unique. Some people made fun of him, but I liked him, and we became friends." Rett, our more reserved grandson, didn't go into a lot of details, he got right to the point. "Mimi, we should be friends with everyone." I hope this teachable moment will lead to others that will move our grandsons toward acts of kindness and care for their peers.

Dick and I would like to ask you to make this personal:

Find a pair of shoes that don't fit your child.

Ask him/her to play in them for a while.

Now have them repeat the activity in their own, well-fitting shoes.

Ask them questions and encourage them to empathize with children who have to wear shoes that don't fit all the time.

Take it a step further with these questions:

Do you know someone in your class who might not feel like they fit in?

How do you think that makes them feel?

Does it make you sad to think of one of your classmates feeling that way?

Can you find a way to help that person feel special and included?

Teach safety

As a caring adult, let's make sure that our children are kept safe from those who might want to harm them, especially when it comes to Internet use. Please ensure that these BIG THREE recommendations are followed as you maintain safety for your children:

The big three:

1. Have consistent "safe" conversations about Internet dangers, safe sites, and unsafe chat rooms.

2. Keep the computer in a well-trafficked area in the home, never in the child's room.

3. Maintain access to your child's emails and social media.

For more details, become educated by reviewing this website and putting these suggestions into practice: http://www.cyberpatrol.com/home/customer-care/online-safety-tips.aspx.

ONE SPARK CAN
SET THE WORLD
ON FIRE

*The tipping point is that magic moment when an
idea, trend, or social behavior crosses a threshold,
tips, and spreads like wildfire.*
—MALCOLM GLADWELL

MAKING A DIFFERENCE doesn't have to be on a grand scale, giving millions of dollars or serving in front of an adoring audience. After all, even a giant redwood tree starts out as a minuscule seed, but when it's mature, its roots extend deep and wide, cementing its place for the ages. It's often those tiny acts of kindness and service that plant seeds that bear fruit over time, pollinating lives and organizations further than the planter knows.

That's how I imagine the life of Martha Jeane Giglio. She was well into her seventies when I first met her, a rail-thin woman with stylish glasses. She had a smile that lit up her whole face, which was rimmed in pale, blonde-grey hair, with cornflower-blue eyes that seemed to seek out only the best in other people. When she came for a tour of Wellspring Living with her niece Alice in 2007, she didn't have access to a tremendous fortune, but she offered what she had—her generous heart and her time. "I don't know exactly what I can do, but I have to do something to be involved," she said with conviction. "Sign me up, and I'll be here once a week."

And she was. Often, she brought a friend, someone else with varied life experiences, people who set the kind of example that really made an impact on our program's participants. She herself would sit and talk with the women, whose young lives had been ravaged by exploitation and pain, offering them encouragement, care, life lessons, and love. When her time each week drew to a close, she passed around her trusty Wellspring Notebook, and the girls would write down anything that troubled them or that they were struggling through, with full confidence that Martha Jeane would spend the week praying for them until she arrived at the house the following week, just like clockwork.

Martha Jeane was the matriarch of an incredible family, and she often spoke with pride of the leadership of her son, Louie, who was, at the time, becoming renowned as an international leader of college students and their parents, and of her daughter, Gina, who cares for people in her own reach with fervor and passion.

In addition, she spoke with such love and affection of her spectacular daughter-in-law, Shelley. I believe she knew that Shelley would carry on her legacy. No one realized how Martha Jeane's seemingly small interactions with the women of Wellspring Living would not only be carried on, but expanded beyond anyone's expectations through Shelley.

Now I am proud to call Shelley my friend, and it's been a pleasure to watch her kernels of ideas grow into a movement that is truly making world-changing waves. Here's her story, in her own eloquent words.

Shelley's Story:

Let me start by saying that everything starts small. Companies start small. Ideas begin as just a thought. And movements can be birthed as the embryo of a cause that one person is passionate about. It's easy to look at something that's already huge, assume it started that way, and get discouraged. Here's how my story went—believe me, it started small and has grown beyond my wildest imagination.

I grew up in Houston, Texas, the second child in an oil family. While we weren't overly spoiled or indulged, we had a great life, and I didn't lack anything. My parents modeled the importance of faith and showed me by example that going against the grain in order to do the right thing was one of the best qualities a person could possess.

I enrolled at Baylor University in Waco, Texas, in 1982, studying business, with a focus in marketing and management. When I went home to Houston that summer, this energetic, twentysomething guy was the college pastor intern at my church. His name was Louie Giglio, and as we got to know each other over the ensuing months, we both knew that we were going to spend the rest of our lives serving people together.

We married in 1986, the year I finished school, and decided to stay on the Baylor campus to work with college students. We had an inkling that capturing young, still-forming hearts was one of the best ways to set them on a course for great things in life. We started Choice, a small gathering. In fact, "small" might be too grand a word. When it started, "tiny" might be more accurate. At first, just a precious few students attended each week, and we talked about life, choices, God, and the world. Over the next ten years, we saw the gathering grow to nearly fifteen hundred each week—about 10 percent of the university's students. That experience on campus cemented a passion in our hearts for college-aged young adults at one of their most compelling stages of life.

Louie's father was ill, though, and had been for some time, so we made plans to move to Atlanta to help his mother. We purposefully handed over Choice to the next crop of leaders at Baylor, not exactly sure what we would do in Georgia. Sadly, though, his dad (Louie, Jr.) passed away before our moving vans made it to town. On what was supposed to be our last day in Waco, at an event honoring our ten-year investment at Baylor, we were in Atlanta, at Louie Jr.'s funeral. Our hearts were broken, but we learned an important lesson: sometimes you have to leave where you are, where you're comfortable and familiar, to get where you're going and ultimately where you're meant to be. For us, tragedy and loss paved the way for something brand-new, though we didn't yet know what that would be.

It was 1995, and later that year, Louie told me that he had a vision for doing something big with college students, something that would inspire them to change the world. In fact, to hear him tell it, it was a flash, a picture in his mind, seen for only the briefest of seconds before it was gone, so quickly that he questioned if he'd really seen it. Yet it was so big, he was confident that only God—this great, big, creative God we serve—could have revealed it. It took him days to even share it with me, because he wanted to discern if it was really supposed to be our next step.

As soon as he told me, though, I knew. I mean, I really knew that God could do anything. It always strikes me as amazing that we are paired up as a team, a study in opposites, so very, very different in personality and approach. Louie has great vision, and my contribution is often a small seed of faith

---

We started calling homeless shelters and asked what they most needed.

---

that his vision can and will become a reality.

In 1996, we connected with like-minded campus leaders around the country to plan. In January of 1997, we held the first Passion conference in Austin, Texas, with two thousand college students in attendance. Many of them were friends of friends of ours and came simply by virtue of the strong relationships on college campuses we'd built over the years. It was smaller than Louie's vision, but it was only the start.

That first conference paved the way for the first decade of Passion, where worship increasingly became a centerpiece of the vision. In 2006, we began to take a closer look at worship in the church and the other side of that same coin: justice. It was all fine and well to sing songs and instill truth into college students, but we couldn't close our eyes to the injustice going on all around us. So we started to prioritize serving and loving the marginalized, and using our lives in such a way that would fuel justice around the world. We used to laugh and say, "However many thousands of people at Passion shouldn't be together without the city being changed. The city should *feel* it."

We started by calling homeless shelters and asked what they most needed. They said towels and socks. So we started asking college students to bring those items and as a result, homeless shelters in "Passion cities" have had their closets filled to the brim. It wasn't a challenging request, but it could have been life changing to someone on the street who needed those things most.

In 2008, we launched the Passion Global Tour, visiting seventeen cities in sixteen countries, each of which had near-sold-out venues of mammoth proportions. We've held conferences in Sydney, Cape Town, Kiev, Manila, Kuala Lumpur, Vancouver, and many more, and as the conferences have grown, we've put an even greater focus on other important issues impacting our world. Clean drinking water, education, and freedom have all become causes we care deeply about.

I thought, *I know I won't have the opportunity to change all this, but I bet I could change something.*

One of the most memorable moments on this journey for me was being in Haiti. Even before the 2010 earthquake, it was one of the most impoverished places I'd ever seen. In fact, I don't think I've ever witnessed that magnitude of poverty and desperation. The intensity is turned up so high there, so it's almost as if your eyes never get to rest. Everywhere you look they're taking in something more tragic than the last glimpse. I remember thinking, *I know I won't have the opportunity to change all this, but I bet I could change something.*

Not long after, I remember the first time we talked about sex trafficking at a Passion conference. The students were shocked that that sort of atrocity was still rampant in our world, even in the United States. I'll never forget the murmur of understanding that reverberated around a packed auditorium like shock waves as they really got it. It's caused a huge ripple.

In 2013 the Passion conference garnered national attention as attendees gave over $3 million in four days to help fund the freedom fight for the estimated 27 million human slaves currently being exploited around the world. This proves that once people—

especially motivated college students—understand a problem, they have to be part of the solution. You cannot walk away; you're compelled to act.

It *is* making a difference. We met Lilia in the Philippines through an organization Passion's students helped fund. As just a young girl, she was discovered in 2008 being forced to work in a brothel against her will. Through the program, she received the treatment and resources she needed and was strong enough, in 2012, to testify in court. The traffickers were convicted and are serving life sentences in tough Philippine prisons. These days, she owns a small general store and is building her life of freedom.

Of course, that's just one story of one survivor, one life changed, but there are countless stories of college students whose lives were also drastically redirected. We've realized that the university age is so critical for deciding the template of what life will be. Most of us have grown up under our parents' systems and culture—from lifestyle to religion to expectations. When you're eighteen to around twenty-five, the world in most cases is open to you. Young adults have many choices and are deciding what they will do with their lives. We want to be one of the voices in that time period to speak into them—and encourage them to leverage their lives to impact other people. We want them to be part of the bigger story.

We can't control a lot of things in life, but we can control our willingness to act. Believe me, I've found it's always worth it.

It's undeniable that Shelley's life is making a difference. She influences people through worship music by well-known artists like Chris Tomlin, Crowder, and Matt Redman, whom her label, sixstepsrecords, produces and manages. I personally can attest to Shelley's unique gift of leadership. She can lead thousands, maybe millions, of people across the globe, but she also ignites individual passions. Recently, Shelley initiated a monthly women's gathering, the GROVE, and our staff felt this Monday night event would be an encouragement for the girls and women we served. From its inception, Wellspring Living staff, women, and girls have traveled over an hour in Atlanta traffic to join thousands of other women from diverse backgrounds seeking inspiration. Time and time again, the girls and women individually shared things like, "When I go to the GROVE, I find myself looking to Shelley as a champion for me" and "I believe even though she hasn't met me, she is my friend."

In addition, Passion conferences around the world have Shelley's fingerprints all over them. She helps shape lives and birth dreams in those she mentors and meets, encouraging everyone around her to pursue making a difference in their own spheres, be they big or small.

Shelley Giglio is truly one of a kind. So was her mother-in-law, Martha Jeane, who prayed for and loved the women of Wellspring Living right up until the day she passed from this life into the next.

ONE CHALLENGE

Kids who need love the most will ask for it
in the most unloving of ways.
—RUSSELL A. BARKLEY

THE CHALLENGE

THE ABOVE QUOTE couldn't be more accurate. Children who especially need our love and attention can't express it in ways that we adults recognize.

Most of the time, they seek love through defiant behavior or quiet withdrawal. To embrace a movement of safeguarding every child is truly a challenge. It will require more resources than you have, more love than you imagined, and probably more patience than you've ever extended. I believe we can all agree that every child should be given the opportunity to reach his or her potential. We can no longer ignore the ones who are in desperate and dangerous circumstances or think someone else is going to take care of it. There are simply too many children requiring caring adults to maintain this mindset.

> **You can make a difference where you are.**

So now that you know the truth, have seen the impact that acts of kindness have toward children, and have witnessed the forever transformation of lives as a result of care and attention, let me ask you: Have you been challenged to do something for one child, one family, or even more than one? I believe that massive intentional living with eyes alerted to children around us and loving care could drastically change our world.

As I face the overwhelming numbers of at-risk children, I become paralyzed. I am persuaded that neither I nor anyone else, can do this alone. We must gather our friends, houses of faith, neighbors, circles of influence, our companies, our civic groups, and our service organizations and work together and create solutions.

You've read on these pages stories of many "ones": ones who, learning of a need, reacted and stepped up—often joining other "ones" to make a difference in the lives of countless individuals.

And so can you. Whether you have a following of thousands or a connection with just one person in need, make a difference where you are. You never know how that one spark of kindness can shape the future.

ONE HOPE

And so Lord, where do I put my hope?
My only hope is in you.
—PSALM 39:7 (NLT)

WHEN WE THINK OF A "ZERO" MOVEMENT, it's clear that this idea didn't originate with us or any other human. From the beginning of time, God longed to draw all people into a relationship with Him. Throughout the Bible, we find evidence of God's desire for us to come close, so He could make all things right, taking the first step toward us.

He makes a beautiful promise in Jeremiah 29:13–14, saying, "'You will seek me and find me when you seek me with all your heart. I will be found by you,' declares the Lord." This is the Lord's desire—that we seek Him and find Him.

How do we do that? First, we acknowledge that something in us is broken, something has broken our relationship with God, who is absolutely perfect. "In him there is no darkness at all" (1 John 1:5).

We then believe that He made the way for us to be reconciled to Him. He offered His own Son, Jesus, as the needed sacrifice for our sins. This is what Jesus Christ's death on the cross is all about. Rather than our trying to make up for our sins and trying to be better and better and "more good," He took our sin on Himself and paid for it once and for all. He offers us His salvation as a gift, not something we need to earn.

Do you believe this? Have you received this gift? "To all who did receive him, to those who believed in his name, he gave the right to become children of God" (John 1:12).

You've read in these pages the need for change in our culture and the part each of us can have in effecting change. The reality is that all our attempts won't be enough to turn the tide to create a safer world for our children. We need a power greater than ourselves; we need God's help. And He is our "ever-present help in trouble" (Psalm 46:1).

Our hope for cultural change is rooted in deep faith in God. My (Mary Frances) faith journey began early in life. As a child, I believed and held John 3:16, a familiar verse from the Bible, close to my heart. It says, "For God so loved the world that he gave his one and only Son, that whoever believes in him shall not perish but have eternal life." My journey began filled with joy to know God loved me and through Jesus, I would never be alone. Even as an eight-year-old girl, I experienced a sweet freedom and a fresh excitement toward life.

But like many who come to faith as a child, I responded to my newfound faith in the only way I knew and became a "good girl," following religious practices. It wasn't the way God intended our relationship to go, because I didn't experience the adventure of really knowing God. I didn't understand the most important principle of the character and intention of God for me. You see, God made us for a relationship with Him, not to simply become religious. It wasn't until I went through my own deep valley of pain that my faith became real and vibrant.

I (Jennifer), similarly, expressed faith when I was a tiny child of six, drawn to this loving Jesus who gave His very life for me. My parents modeled God's love, and it was easy to believe that God is good and is for me. The storms of life came quickly, though, and my father passed away when I was eleven, making my mother a widow at just thirty-four. I knew intimately what it was like to be fatherless, but I also experienced the truth of Romans 10:11–13, which says, "Scripture reassures us, 'No one who trusts God like this—heart and soul—will ever regret it.' It's exactly the same no matter what a person's religious background may be: the same God for all of us, acting the same incredibly generous way to everyone who calls out for help. Everyone who calls, 'Help, God!' gets help" (MSG).

For both of us, through walking different, difficult paths, the Bible stories have become real and we, individually, experienced the *why* of faith. Through Jesus, God shows His heart for everyone—especially those whom the world doesn't see. Jesus was always on the lookout for the forgotten: the children, the poor, and even the prostitutes. Jesus looked beyond what was seen outwardly and saw the person he or she could become.

We couldn't complete this book without confirming the fuel

behind our passion for every child to be safeguarded. It's God's love planted deeply in our hearts and our belief in Jesus that turns faith into compassionate action. Paul, one of the Bible's writers, expressed it so well in Galatians 5:6: "The only thing that counts is faith expressing itself through love."

God created each of us with unique personalities and abilities that only He can bring out to impact in the world. God also gives us—and all who believe—hope that He can multiply our efforts to truly make a positive change in the world.

As pastor and author Andy Stanley reminds us, "Something inside us hopes for the possibility that everything in our lives, even our worst moments, can be made right, that we can be redeemed."

We couldn't agree more. We all need redemption—whether you are a successful business leader, a homeless person, a political activist, a hungry mom, an orphan, a humanitarian leader, a lonely teen, a faith leader, or an exploited child—we were meant for a higher purpose.

Let us first seek God and find Him, through Jesus Christ His Son. Once we have God's heart inside our heart, we will be empowered with strength beyond ourselves to unite, to become more resourceful to maintain the work, more loving than could be imagined, display more patience than ever extended. We'll do this together so that every child is safeguarded and the number of at risk children can be reduced to zero.

To learn more about the message of salvation as explained in the Bible, please call 1-888-NEED-HIM or visit https://needhim.org/.

—MARY FRANCES BOWLEY AND
JENNIFER BRADLEY FRANKLIN

CONNECT WITH US AT:
twitter.com/makeitzerobook
facebook.com/makeitzerobook
instagram.com/makeitzerobook

Notes

PART ONE: ZERO POVERTY

1. American Community Survey (ACS) 2009–2013.
2. Annie E. Casey Foundation (AECF) "Encyclopedia of Quality of Life and Well-Being Research 2014. http://www.aecf.org/m/resourcedoc/aecf-2014kidscountdata-book-2014.pdf.
3. Ibid.

PART TWO: ZERO HUNGER

1. World Hunger. www.worldhunger.org.
2. http://www.ers.usda.gov/media/1565415/err173.pdf.
3. Feeding America, *Key Findings*. http://www.feedingamerica.org/.
4. Share Our Strength: https://www.nokidhungry.org/the-problem.

PART THREE: ZERO ISOLATION

1. Annie E. Casey Foundation, 13.
2. Ibid.
3. Ibid.
4. Ibid., 17.
5. Connection Homes, *Aging Out.* connectionhomes.org/programs/aging-out-of-foster-care-2/.
6. *Merriam-Webster Dictionary.*
7. American Humane Association. www.americanhumane.org.
8. Wess Stafford, *Just a Minute: In the Heart of a Child, One Moment . . . Can Last Forever* (Chicago: Moody, 2012), 14.
9. C. C. Barber, P. Fonagy, J. Fultz, M. Simulinas, and M. Yates, "Homeless Near a Thousand Homes: Outcomes of Homeless Youth in a Crisis Shelter," *American Journal of Orthopsychiatry*, 75, (2005): 347–55.
10. E. A. Eastwood and J. M. Birnbaum, "Physical and Sexual Abuse and Unstable Housing among Adolescents with HIV," *AIDS and Behavior*, vol. 11 (2007): Supplement 2: S116–S127.

PART FOUR: ZERO ABUSE

1. http://www.acf.hhs.gov/sites/default/files/cb/cm2012.pdf.
2. Child Abuse Statistics & Facts, www.childhelp.org., citing http://www.acf.hhs.gov/programs/cb/resource/child-maltreatment-2012.
3. Child Abuse Statistics & Facts, www.childhelp.org., citing D. Brown et. al., "Adverse Childhood Experiences and the Risk of Premature Mortality," *American Journal of Preventative Medicine*, vol. 37 (2009): iss. 5.
4. Child Abuse Statistics & Facts, www.childhelp.org., citing http://www.cdc.gov/violenceprevention/acestudy/#1.
5. Child Abuse Statistics & Facts, www.childhelp.org., citing atacenter.kidscount.org/data/tables/6220-children-who-are-subject-to-an-investigated-report?loc=1&loct=2#detailed/1/any/false/867,133,38,35,18/any/12940,12955 and http://www.gao.gov/products/GAO-11-599.

6. http://www.merriam-webster.com/dictionary/abuse.
7. http://www.noexcuse4childabuse.org/community-education/communityeducation .html.
8. Referenced in http://www.ted.com/talks/nadine_burke_harris_how_childhood _trauma_affects_health_across_a_lifetime?language=en.
9. L. J. Lederer and C. A. Wetzel, "The Health Consequences of Sex Trafficking and Their Implications for Identifying Victims in Facilities," *The Annals of Health Law*, 23(1) (2014): 61–91.
10. A. Silverman, H. Reinherz, R. Giaconia, The Long-Term Sequelae of Child and Adolescent Abuse: A Longitudinal Community Study: August, 1996. Retrieved August 20, 2015.
11. http://www.universitypsychiatry.com/clientuploads/pes/Silverman_ CAaN_1996_20_709.pdf.
12. http://www.bjs.gov/content/pub/pdf/saycrle.pdf.

PART FIVE: ZERO TRAFFICKING

1. http://www.ejournalncrp.org/human-trafficking-foster-children-in-l-a/.
2. http://www.ecpatusa.org/statistics.
3. Polaris Project, *Sex Trafficking in the U.S.* www.polarisproject.org.
4. The Shapiro Group, "Men Who Buy Sex with Adolescent Girls: a Scientific Research Study," Atlanta, GA: The Shapiro Group, 2009.
5. Definition of sex trafficking according to the federal Trafficking Victims Protection Act.

RESOURCES FOR FURTHER INSIGHT
Poverty

TED TALK

Gary Haugen, founder of International Justice Mission, talks about the things we don't know about poverty: https://www.ted.com/talks/gary_haugen_the_hidden_reason_for _poverty_the_world_needs_to_address_now.

BOOKS

Donna Beegle, *See Poverty . . . Be the Difference* (Portland, OR: Communication Across Barriers, Inc., 2007).

Maria Cancian and Sheldon Danziger, eds., *Changing Poverty, Changing Policies* (Russell Sage Foundation, 2009).

Peter Edelman, *So Rich, So Poor: Why It's So Hard to End Poverty in America* (New York: The New Press, 2013).

Ron Hall, *Same Kind of Different as Me* (Nashville: Thomas Nelson, 2006).

David T. Williams, *Christian Approaches to Poverty* (Lincoln, NE: Authors Choice Press, 2001).

REPORTS

Donna Beegle, "Breaking Poverty Barriers to Equal Justice," http://news.nasje.org/wp-content/uploads/2010/10/CR-03a-Breaking-Barriers_Beegle_EQUAL-JUSTICE LEGAL-PRO.pdf.

Donna Beegle, "Interrupting Generational Poverty: Factors Influencing Successful Completion of the Bachelor's Degree," Doctoral Dissertation, Portland State University, 2000, http://www.combarriers.com/pdf/TP0151Overcoming.pdf.

WEBSITES

www.povertyusa.org

"What Money": an activity for better understanding limited resources—www.combarriers.com

HUNGER

TED TALK

Josette Sheeran, head of the UN's World Food Program, on Ending Hunger Now: http://www.ted.com/talks/josette_sheeran_ending_hunger_now

BOOKS

Joel Berg, *All You Can Eat: How Hungry Is America?* (New York: Seven Stories Press, 2011).

Jonathan Bloom, *American Wasteland: How America Throws Away Nearly Half of Its Food (and What We Can Do About It)* (Cambridge, MA: Da Capo Press, 2013).

Megan A. Carney, *The Unending Hunger: Tracing Women and Food Insecurity across Borders* (Oakland, CA: University of California Press, 2015).

Peter Pringle, ed., *A Place at the Table: The Crisis of 49 Million Hungry Americans and How to Solve It* (New York: Public Affairs, 2013).

WEBSITES

www.feedingamerica.org
www.nokidhungry.org

ISOLATION

TED TALK

Experienced educator Rita Pierson, "Every Kid Needs a Champion": http://www.ted.com/talks/rita_pierson_every_kid_needs_a_champion

BOOKS

Tom Davis, *Fields of the Fatherless* (Colorado Springs: David C. Cook, 2008).

Kathleen Nader, *Understanding and Assessing Trauma in Children and Adolescents: Measures, Methods, and Youth in Context* (New York: Routledge, 2008).

Pam Parish, *Ready or Not* (Atlanta: Ready or Not Resources, 2014).

WEBSITES

www.nctsn.org

http://everydaylife.globalpost.com/effects-isolation-childs-social-development-5491.html

www.childwelfare.gov

ARTICLE

Frances Kemper Alston, Latch-Key Children http://www.education.com/reference/article/Ref_Latch_Key_Children/

ABUSE

TED TALK

Pediatrician Nadine Burke Harris discusses childhood trauma and health: http://www.ted.com/talks/nadine_burke_harris_how_childhood_trauma_affects_health_across_a_lifetime?language=en

BOOKS

Dan Allender, *The Wounded Heart: Hope for Adult Victims of Childhood Sexual Abuse* (Colorado Springs: NavPress, 2013).

Nicole Braddock Bromley, *Breathe: Finding Freedom to Thrive in Relationships after Childhood Sexual Abuse* (Chicago: Moody, 2009).

Nicole Braddock Bromley, *Hush: Moving from Silence to Healing after Childhood Sexual Abuse* (Chicago: Moody, 2007).

Robyn MacBridge, *Sexual Abuse—Child Sexual Abuse True Stories (What You Need to Know & Shocking Child Abuse Statistics)* (CreateSpace, 2013).

Sheri Oz and Sarah-Jane Ogiers, *Overcoming Childhood Sexual Trauma: A Guide to Breaking Through the Wall of Fear for Practitioners and Survivors* (New York: Routledge, 2014). Available online.

Chris Trotter, *Helping Abused Children and Their Families* (Thousand Oaks, CA: SAGE Publications, 2004).

WEBSITES

http://www.d2l.org

http://www.missingkids.com/Runaway

www.childhelp.org

www.futureswithoutviolence.org

http://www.childabuse.org

TRAFFICKING

TED TALKS

Mary Frances Bowley, founder of Wellspring Living, "On the Brink": https://www.youtube.com/watch?v=NqqhjaBkPgc

Resources

Kevin Bales, cofounder of Free the Slaves on "How to Combat Modern Slavery" http://www.ted.com/talks/kevin_bales_how_to_combat_modern_slavery?language=en

Nacole, mother of four on "Child Sex Trafficking in America": https://www.youtube.com/watch?v=C7EbFtg8ALk

DOCUMENTARY
http://www.inplainsightfilm.com/Documentary of Sex Trafficking in America

WEBSITES
www.traffickingresourcecenter.org

www.polarisproject.org

www.wellspringliving.org

www.inplainsight.com

BOOKS
Mary Frances Bowley, *The White Umbrella* (Chicago: Moody, 2012).

Mary de Chesnay, *Sex Trafficking: A Clinical Guide for Nurses* (New York: Springer Publishing Company, 2013).

Linda Smith, *Renting Lacy: A Story of America's Prostituted Children; A Call to Action* (Vancouver, WA: Shared Hope International, 2013).

CONNECT WITH US AT:
twitter.com/makeitzerobook
facebook.com/makeitzerobook
instagram.com/makeitzerobook

JENNIFER BRADLEY FRANKLIN is a multi-platform journalist and editor, specializing in travel, food, and lifestyles. Her work appears in *USA Today, Delta SKY, American Way, People, Food Network*, and a host of others. She holds an ABJ in journalism from the University of Georgia's Grady College. Jennifer has ridden a camel in Morocco, dug ditches in a remote Kenyan village, been taught to make gnocchi by a master chef in Florence, and learned to surf in Australia. However, one of her greatest joys has been immersing herself in some of the biggest concerns facing America's young people—weighty issues like poverty, hunger, and much more—through the research and writing of *Make It Zero*. Follow her on Instagram and Twitter @JennBFranklin and learn more at www.jenniferbradleyfranklin.com.

MARY FRANCES BOWLEY has always had a passion for children, especially the ones others didn't see, which led to her teaching for fifteen years. Through several eye-opening experiences, Mary Frances launched Wellspring Living in 2001, an organization caring for exploited young women and girls. Working with countless girls and women revealed deeper issues preceding exploitation. Their stories must be told. To ensure that readers would be compelled to action, she enlisted Jennifer Bradley Franklin. Jennifer is a writer and journalist, specializing in travel, food, beauty, fashion, news, and profiles. However, Mary Frances discovered Jennifer's dynamic storytelling abilities and believed she was the perfect one to bring life to *Make It Zero*. Through the writing of *Make It Zero,* a beautiful friendship developed. The flow of their words creates a rallying call for every reader to unite to reduce the number of at-risk children to ZERO.

Sex trafficking.

We often hear about it from afar, but it occurs daily in our own communities. The author of *Make It Zero*, Mary Frances Bowley, shares stories that describe the pain and strength of survivors as well as stories of those who hold the "white umbrella" of protection and purity over them. See the need for these protecting, caring partners, and learn what it means to love and care for survivors in action, prayer, and support.

MOODY
Publishers™

From the Word to Life

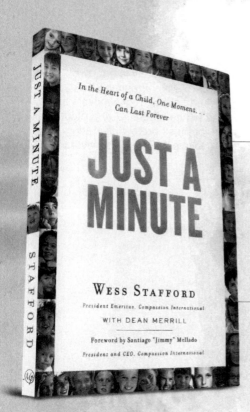

68 STORIES THAT WILL INSPIRE YOU TO BLESS A CHILD'S LIFE

Individual moments in a young person's life can make all the difference in their future. Read story after powerful story of lives changed because someone took just a minute to connect in the life of a child. Stay alert— you never know when your opportunity will come.

MOODY
Publishers™

*From the Word **to** Life*

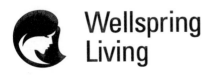

Wellspring Living

to live and dream again

Wellspring Living is devoted to safeguarding and empowering domestic sex trafficking victims and those at risk. Through life-giving residential and community-based programs, girls (12-17) and young women (18-32) are provided the opportunity to live and dream again.

OUR MISSION IS TO HELP DOMESTIC SEX TRAFFICKING VICTIMS AND THE VULNERABLE DEVELOP THE COURAGE TO MOVE FORWARD AND THE CONFIDENCE TO SUCCEED

WellspringLiving.org

Facebook.com/WellspringLiving

Twitter.com/WellspringLivin

Instagram.com/WellspringLivin

Youtube.com/user/wellspringliving

MOODY
Radio™

*From the Word **to Life***

Moody Radio produces and delivers compelling programs filled with biblical insights and creative expressions of faith that help you take the next step in your relationship with Christ.

You can hear Moody Radio on 36 stations and more than 1,500 radio outlets across the U.S. and Canada. Or listen on your smartphone with the Moody Radio app!

www.moodyradio.org